THE SOURCE OF MY STRENGTH

THE SOURCE OF MY STRENGTH

CHARLES STANLEY

THOMAS NELSON PUBLISHERS
Nashville • Atlanta • London • Vancouver

Published in Nashville, Tennessee, by Thomas Nelson, Inc., Publishers, and distributed in
Canada by Word Communications, Ltd., Richmond, British Columbia.

Unless otherwise noted, the Bible version used in this publication is THE NEW KING
JAMES VERSION. Copyright © 1979, 1980, 1982, Thomas Nelson, Inc., Publishers.

Printed in the United States of America.

Library of Congress Cataloging-in-Publication Data

Stanley, Charles F.
      The source of my strength / Charles Stanley.
         p.   cm.
      ISBN 0-7852-8273-4
      1. Suffering—Religious aspects—Christianity.   2. Consolation.
   3. Holy Spirit.   4. Liberty—Religious aspects—Christianity.
   5. Stanley, Charles F.   I. Title.
   BV4909.S73   1994
   248.8′6—dc20   93-48445
                                                                              CIP

              5   6 — 99   98   97   96   95   94

CONTENTS

Introduction: Setting Down Our Emotional Baggage   *1*

----

*Words of
Comfort
and
Healing
to . . .*

1. Those who are LONELY   *9*
2. Those who are FEARFUL   *29*
3. Those who are suffering from ABUSE   *67*
4. Those who are feeling INFERIOR   *91*
5. Those who are struggling under the weight of GUILT   *117*
6. Those who are FRUSTRATED   *139*
7. Those who are BURNED OUT   *187*
8. Those who are being PERSECUTED   *215*

Conclusion: The Purifying Power of Pain   *237*

The Spirit of the LORD is upon Me,
Because He has anointed Me
To preach the gospel to the poor;
He has sent Me to heal the brokenhearted,
To proclaim liberty to the captives
And recovery of sight to the blind,
To set at liberty those who are oppressed;
To proclaim the acceptable year of the LORD.
       —Luke 4:18–19

Setting Down Our Emotional Baggage

O ne of the most powerful statements that Jesus ever made was that He came "to seek and to save that which was lost" (Luke 19:10). For many years, that was the most important statement of the Lord in my personal life, and it was on that word that I based my ministry.

In recent years, however, I have discovered another statement of Jesus for which I am equally grateful:

> The Spirit of the LORD is upon Me,
> Because He has anointed Me
> To preach the gospel to the poor;
> He has sent Me to heal the brokenhearted,
> To proclaim liberty to the captives
> And recovery of sight to the blind,
> To set at liberty those who are oppressed (Luke 4:18).

When I began to discover that Jesus Christ came not only to take care of my sin problem but to make me a whole

1

person, something truly wonderful happened in my life. It is the reason I am writing this book today. I hope and pray that you, too, will come to experience the "Spirit of the LORD," be set free of the past, and be made whole in Christ.

No matter who we are today, we are "poor"—or lacking —in some way. We are brokenhearted over something or someone. We are captives to the memories of the past and the limited expectations we have for our futures. We are blind to our true position and place in the Lord Jesus Christ. We truly need to be set free because each of us is oppressed by the enemy of the soul.

Some of the heartaches, afflictions, and trials in our lives stem from external causes; others stem from internal causes. Regardless of their origin, however, the pains are real. And unless we are willing to deal with the painful experiences that life brings our way, the pain becomes a "burden and wound" of the heart. Afflictions turn into damaged feelings, hurts turn into habitual patterns of behavior that are destructive, failures and rejection result in a flawed outlook on the world and on God, and harmful and destructive relationships become a heaviness deep within that keeps us from truly experiencing the fullness of freedom and purpose that the Lord has for us.

EMOTIONAL BAGGAGE BECOMES BONDAGE

Emotional baggage is the term I use to refer to those feelings, thought patterns, and past experiences that continue to traumatize a person each time they are triggered or recalled, and that affect in an ongoing way a person's behavior and responses to life.

Emotional baggage keeps a person in spiritual bondage. It weighs down a person with guilt, pain, and inner suffering. Such emotional baggage

◆ keeps a person from being the kind of person God wants the individual to be.

◆ keeps a person from doing what God calls the individual to do.

◆ keeps a person paralyzed with doubt, fear, and self-recrimination.

◆ keeps a person from developing a healthy self-image.

Some of this baggage is so heavy that a person must deal with it in order to be able to cope with life on a daily basis. Some of the baggage seems so light that it doesn't really interfere with normal daily relationships and responsibilities. The wise person will deal with emotional baggage, no matter how heavy or light it may be.

Why?

Because emotional baggage ultimately keeps a person from experiencing the freedom that Christ Jesus longs to give. And life is at its best when a person is free!

WHY HANG ON TO THE PAINFUL PAST?

It takes courage to put down emotional baggage.

Some people get so used to living with baggage that they feel threatened at the very thought of laying it down. They are so accustomed to living with pain that they can't imagine life without pain. Let me assure you today, life is *better* without the weight of emotional baggage pulling at your soul.

Some people feel guilty at laying down their past. They seem to feel as if they are also laying down the validity of past relationships or that they are, in some way, hurting the people they are forgiving, forgetting, or releasing. If that is your fear today, let me assure you that Jesus Christ will free you from all guilt, and in your letting go of the past, you will also be freeing Him to do His full work in that other person's life. The best thing that you can do for yourself and for the person who has abandoned you, rejected you, or abused you is to turn the person over to God and let Him deal with the person.

Still other people don't want to face what they perceive will be a struggle or a painful process involved in setting down their emotional baggage. Although it is true that releasing emotional baggage sometimes brings us to the point of tears, those tears quickly turn to tears of rejoicing. There is nothing as comforting, encouraging, uplifting, or joyful as casting off the weight of emotional baggage and walking freely in life.

There is no benefit in continuing to carry emotional burdens. There is no good reason for hanging on to what slows you down, keeps you from feeling free, or stops you from experiencing the fullness of the life that God has prepared for you to live.

LIGHTENING THE LOAD

On a recent trip to the High Sierra mountain range of California, I became aware of something obvious that I had never really noticed before. The pack animals that carried us and our gear had no way of freeing themselves from the burdens on their backs. The heavy loads they carried had to be removed by one of us human beings making the trek.

The same principle holds true for us as we bear the weight of our emotional baggage. As important as it is for us to lay down emotional baggage, we cannot do so on our own strength or ability.

Neither does emotional baggage drift away or disappear over time. I've met people who have carried very heavy emotional baggage for decades and decades. If time resolved the problem of emotional baggage, there would be no emotional baggage! Further, true freedom and release are possible only in Christ Jesus. As John 8:36 tells us so succinctly, "If the Son makes you free, you shall be free indeed."

And what of those spiritual burdens that we may believe the Lord has laid on our hearts? We can always be assured that if the Lord causes a heaviness to enter our hearts in order to direct us toward the Lord's will or to guide our prayers of intercession toward another person, those heartfelt burdens are nearly always short-lived, and they never tear us down, destroy our ability to function in life, haunt us, or damage our feelings of self-value.

The same holds for valleys or wilderness times. We go through down periods in which we suffer in our emotions.

No person can live a life free of all problems, pain, trouble, or difficulty. Problems are unavoidable.

When seen from the Lord's perspective, however, the purpose of the valleys is that we might be *outfitted*—equipped, prepared, strengthened—for the climb to the top of the mountain, which is where the Lord is always seeking to lead us. Valleys and wilderness times in which we may feel isolated or tested are never permanent.

Oswald Chambers in the book *So Send I You* writes of "the vision, the valley, and the verity." God gives us a vision and then puts us in the valley in order to sift us, sand us, discipline us, prune us—in other words, to rid us of all that would be a hindrance to us in climbing up to or living on top of the mountain. It is in the valley that we make a decision to leave the valley and climb up the mountain God has set before us.

Furthermore, even in these times we may regard as discouraging or rugged, the Lord's desire is that we be truly free in the inner person. The freedom is not external. It is internal. It is freedom in our hearts even as we face trials and adversities.

THE COURAGE TO TAKE THE FIRST STEP

Even with full recognition that the definitive removal of emotional baggage requires the aid of the Lord Jesus, we must also recognize that setting down our emotional baggage takes an act of the will to turn to the Lord for His help.

The Lord will not strip us of our painful memories or our hurtful experiences unless we ask Him to do so.

He will not heal us of our withered mental attitudes unless we request it of Him.

The Lord will not invade our hearts and transform our natures unless we invite Him in and request Him to heal us and make us whole.

Getting free requires an act of the human will. It requires that we choose to turn to the Lord and ask Him to engage in the healing process with us.

Today is a great day to

◆ ask the Lord Jesus to take off your heart the load you are carrying.

◆ ask the Lord to ease your burden.

◆ ask the Lord to free you from the bondage you are in.

And as you ask, trust Him to be faithful to His Word and to free you.

Now some of you may be thinking this is impossible. Friend, don't despair. It is impossible for you to go back and redo or undo whatever happened in the past, but you can confront your past baggage now, in the present. Just as now is where you find the troublesome behavioral and attitudinal by-products in your life, so now is where you can find God's solution.

Healing is to be found in the present—in conversations with caring friends, relatives, and counselors; in reading and meditating on the Bible; in prayer; and, on occasion, by thinking carefully about the past painful circumstances and deliberately placing your gift of forgiveness on those involved. To be sure, you will need God's help to do this, but with His help you will receive healing for your todays.

In the chapters that follow, I use my personal experiences with emotional baggage to illustrate how God can heal your hurts and help you release the past and live fully in the present.

You cannot free yourself. But you can take the first step toward freedom by saying to the Lord today, "Lord, I am trusting You to help me face the emotional baggage I am carrying and to help me have the courage to walk through life without the pain, insecurities, frustrations, and alienation I have been feeling. I am trusting You to free me and then to walk with me as I learn how to live as a free human being and to enter into the full and wonderful life You have planned for me."

*Words
of
comfort
and
healing
to
those
who
are*

LONELY

*T*he scene is etched sharply into my memory. I can see it as clearly today as the day it happened.

Two of my friends—Jimmy and Rob—had come to spend some time with me on a Saturday afternoon. We had laughed and talked and played games together, and then the father of one of the boys came to pick them up in his car.

As I stood in the yard and watched the three of them drive away down the street, a sickening, sinking feeling hit the pit of my stomach. I clearly remember thinking, *I have nobody.*

> *I* clearly remember thinking, *I have nobody.* A feeling of utter loneliness welled up in me—a feeling that was all too familiar. ◆

A feeling of utter loneliness welled up in me—a feeling that was all too familiar, a feeling that had been there for all of my thirteen years.

My very first memory is of sitting up in a bed in a room that had brown boarded walls and was lit by a kerosene lamp. I had a terrible earache. And I was alone.

My father—a worker in a textile mill and the son of a Pentecostal evangelist—died of kidney disease when I was nine months old. At the time, we lived in a little place called Dry Fork, Virginia, just outside Danville. On the Sunday afternoon he passed away, just before he died, my mother asked him, "What will I do if you die?" He replied, "Well, you'll have to do the best you can." His advice sounds cold to me now, but the year was 1933 and probably the only thing that any person could do at that time was "the best you can." For my mother, "doing her best" meant going to work immediately to support the two of us.

Although I do not consciously remember my father's death, I have come to recognize that the little boy in me knew somehow that my father had gone away. In the deepest recesses of my heart I had the knowledge that I had been left alone.

For the first couple of years of my life, various women took care of me while my mother worked. And each day when my mother walked out the door to go to work, the little boy who still lives inside me said, "She's gone. She left you. You are alone."

I remember crying every morning of my fifth year as I prepared to go to school. My mother had to leave early to go to work, so she was always gone by the time I got up. For the first few months of that school year, Uncle Jack came over and helped me get ready for school—he'd comb my hair and cook my breakfast. Before I was out of first grade, however, I had learned to comb my own hair and cook my own breakfast —including an egg and a piece of bacon.

When I came home from school in the afternoon, my mother still wasn't home. She didn't arrive until about five o'clock. Coming home to an empty house really bothered me. It was a constant reminder that I was alone.

I got to the place where I could play all day by myself—riding broomstick horses and playing with toy soldiers. As I got older, I built model airplanes. I had a few friends who would come over to play with me—we could play Monopoly all day—but most of my days were spent by myself. Later, as a teenager, I'd take my .22 down to the creek bank and spend entire afternoons shooting at birds. Alone.

Even during the brief periods through the years when we lived with my aunts and uncles, I suffered from loneliness. My grandparents and uncles would frequently leave my mother and me at home when they'd go out. Although I feel certain now, as an adult, that their leaving us behind was probably a matter of convenience or necessity, as a little boy I saw their leaving as abandonment. I felt it as loneliness.

On one particular Saturday, my mother left our home and didn't return all day. I cried the entire time. I had no idea where she had gone or when she was coming back. Until about three years ago, the loneliest times of my life were Saturday afternoons.

I know I am not alone in my experience.

Although the loneliness of my childhood may be more severe than that experienced by many people, I have met hundreds—even thousands—of people through the years who have felt utterly alone, abandoned, isolated, ostracized, and thus, lonely.

It is one of the most excruciating feelings a person can ever have, and one that nearly every person attempts to avoid at all costs. Those who have spent time in solitary confinement consider it to be one of the worst forms of punishment or imprisonment on earth. They say, for example:

I have met hundreds—even thousands—of people through the years who have felt utterly alone, abandoned, isolated, ostracized, and thus, lonely.

"I can't bear the loneliness. The walls seem to close in on me. The days seem never to end."

"Even when I'm in a crowd, I have this strong sense that I am alone—that nobody really knows I'm there. It's almost as if I'm invisible."

"The day he walked out the door, I thought I'd scream. Not that he was gone. But that he'd left me alone."

"I feel as if I'm swinging my arms in a fog—but rather than connect with anybody, the fog grows thicker."

People who are divorced nearly always give testimony to loneliness. A divorce is an extremely traumatic situation. It literally tears away at the emotions, and very often, the overriding feeling is one of intense loneliness, of being isolated from the rest of the world.

Older people give frequent testimony to loneliness, especially after the death of a spouse. Grief becomes coupled with isolation—an excruciating combination, and sometimes a deadly one. Old friends, old associations, and old responsibilities have sloughed away—leaving only an inner ache for what once was and for friends who are no longer accessible.

Young people cry out in loneliness. Whether latchkey kids or the children of indifferent, self-absorbed parents, our young people frequently speak out about the isolation they feel from peers and from their society as a whole.

Salespeople on the road are lonely.

Mothers of young children and homemakers are lonely.

Those who have moved to new cities and those who have started new jobs are lonely.

College students who are out on their own for the first

time, especially those who have gone away to school, are lonely.

Those who have empty nests after years of raising children are lonely.

Newly retired persons, so accustomed to a wide circle of acquaintances and colleagues, are lonely.

Look around, and you'll find lonely people everywhere.

THE LORD'S RESPONSE

What does our Lord say to people who are lonely?

In the creation story of Genesis 1—3, we have a picture of God desiring the fellowship of human beings. He says, "Let Us make man in Our image, according to Our likeness" (Gen. 1:26)—a likeness complete with an emotional capacity to long for companionship. That desire resident in humankind to seek out God, to long for God in the deep inner recesses of the heart, is mirrored by God's desire for humankind.

Apparently, Adam and Eve walked and talked with God frequently. God's voice to them in the cool of the evening was not strange to them. (See Gen. 3:8–9.)

Time and again throughout the Old Testament, we find the Lord reaching out to His people, revealing Himself to them, desiring to be with them and to communicate with them. In 1 Samuel 12:22, we find this promise of God: "For the LORD will not forsake His people, for His great name's sake, because it has pleased the LORD to make you His people." The Lord's desire is for companionship, fellowship, and communion with those who will respond to Him in like manner.

In the New Testament, we read how Jesus developed a very close relationship with a group of men we call the apostles. He was so concerned that they continue in their relationship with one another even after His crucifixion that He spent much of His last night with them talking about their need to remain one with each other, and to be as one with the Father, just as He was one with them and one with the Father. He promised to send them a Comforter or Helper— the Holy Spirit—who would never leave them and would be not only with them but in them. (See John 14—16.)

The close communion that the Lord desires and is willing to experience with us is something we can count on, even if everyone else abandons us. We see this, too, in the life of Jesus. On the very night He was to be arrested and tried—the trial that would end in His crucifixion—He said to His disciples, "Indeed the hour is coming, yes, has now come, that you will be scattered, each to his own, and will leave Me alone." Can you hear the pain in that statement? Jesus knew what it was to be lonely. But then Jesus went on to say, "And yet I am not alone, because the Father is with Me." Jesus knew what it was to be comforted even in the face of abandonment. (See John 16:32.)

Jesus' final words to His disciples in Matthew 28 were these: "Lo, I am with you always, even to the end of the age." Jesus seemed to have an intense concern that His disciples would know with certainty that the Lord God was closer to them than the very breath that they breathed and that though they would feel lonely at times, they were never actually alone.

The close communion that the Lord desires and is willing to experience with us is something we can count on, even if everyone else abandons us.

Today, Jesus is your Friend of friends. He is one Friend you will always have, who will be "the same yesterday, today, and forever" (Heb. 13:8).

WHEN YOU ARE FEELING LONELY

When loneliness engulfs us, the first thing we must do is to turn our focus away from what we don't have to what we do have. And what do we have? God Himself.

You can't ever be alone once you have trusted in Jesus Christ as your Savior. He says that He comes to dwell within you when you receive Him into your life and that He becomes connected to you just as a vine and a branch are connected. In the same way that sap flows through a vine and its branches, so, too, the love of Christ is flowing in you and through you. He is abiding in you, and you are abiding in Him. You are as one being with Christ. You share with Him the most intimate relationship possible—an eternal spiritual intimacy. (See John 15:1–9.)

The depth of that intimacy is, to a great extent, up to us. It relates to how much we desire to be intimate with the Lord, how much we allow Him to fill us up with His presence, and how willing we are for Him to reveal Himself to us. The fact is, however, that we can never totally isolate ourselves from the Lord. He is always there, desiring to be ever closer to us.

We might ask as the apostle Paul did, "Who shall separate us from the love of Christ? Shall tribulation, or distress, or persecution, or famine, or nakedness, or peril, or sword?"

The answer is also provided by Paul: "For I am persuaded that neither death nor life, nor angels nor principalities nor powers, nor things present nor things to come, nor height nor depth, nor any other created thing, shall be able to separate us from the love of God which is in Christ Jesus our Lord" (Rom. 8:35, 38–39).

You simply cannot be alone once you have the Spirit of God dwelling in you. You can experience a tormenting feeling of emptiness, fear, or desperation. You can feel alone even though you are not alone. These feelings are subject to what you do about them. You can let your feelings drive you away from the Lord—and experience less intimacy with Him. Or you can let these feelings drive you toward the Lord and to an even greater intimacy.

When we choose to turn to the Lord, we are saying to Him, in effect, "I need for You to fill this ache, this void, this loneliness, in my life. I am trusting You to do it. There's nobody else to whom I can turn. I turn completely and to-tally to You." In so doing, we are inviting the Lord to reveal His presence to us—a presence that does, indeed, take away our loneliness.

DON'T SHUT OFF THE WORLD OR SHUT OUT THE LORD

Lonely people sometimes turn to drugs or alcohol to get away from their feelings of loneliness. A chemical-induced lull is never a good substitute for life!

Lonely people may also turn to television, videos, or

radio programs to fill the void of loneliness they feel. While it's true that the media can provide noise in an otherwise quiet house and give a sense of connection with the outside world, it's also true that there are two dangers in turning to a form of the media when one is feeling lonely:

◆ The first danger is that a media form will become a substitute for real-life relationships and involvement in the family or with the greater community in which the person lives. Television isolates a person from the world. It shuts off a person's communication with others and thwarts opportunities to build relationships.

◆ The second danger is that television will become a detour or a diversion that keeps the person from truly turning to the Lord and developing a relationship with Him.

Don't let television, radio, or some other form of media become a cheap substitute for the real thing: a relationship with the Lord and relationships with other people. Rather than watch relationships on television or listen to them on radio, seek to build relationships in real life.

Let me take you back again to the creation story in Genesis. In the first chapter of Genesis, we read how the Lord created the world and all that is in it, and after each act of creation, He says, "It is good." The first time that the Lord says that something is not good is when He addresses the issue of loneliness. The Lord says, "It is not good that man should be alone; I will make him a helper comparable to him" (Gen. 2:18).

The Lord's desire is not only that you have a close, intimate relationship with Him but that you have satisfying and enriching personal relationships with other people. When you are lonely, you turn first to the Lord, but you turn next to people—not to the media or to some type of escapist activity. Loneliness is remedied by interaction and involvement—with the Lord and with others—not by withdrawal or an escape into fantasy or some type of chemical-induced stupor.

One of the greatest blessings in life is a godly friend. Don't be reluctant to call upon such a friend when you experience moments of overwhelming loneliness. That friend is a gift from God to you. This is especially true in times of intense grief over the loss of a loved one or the loss of a relationship. Seek out a friend who will love you, spend time with you, and help you break through the wall of separation you feel from the world.

With television, you have something only for the moment. With other people, you have something that can last a lifetime. With the Lord, you have something that lasts for all eternity.

When you turn off the television set, what do you have? Loneliness again. When you spend time with the Lord, what do you come away with? Feelings of oneness with Him, security, affirmation, encouragement, a sense of His presence and power, a joy in your heart that drives away loneliness.

When you are feeling lonely, first go to the Lord. Say, "Lord, help me to have a relationship with You. I want to know You better. I want to feel Your presence." And then ask the Lord to guide you into satisfying and mutually beneficial relationships with other people. Say to the Lord, "Lord, please provide for me friends who will speak the truth to me and help me to live in a way that is pleasing to You, friends who will love me and who will receive love from me, friends with whom I can share laughter and sorrow, friends with whom I can converse freely." Look for the opportunities to build friendship that the Lord brings your way:

◆ Say yes to social invitations from godly people.

◆ Get involved with your church and with various groups within the church. Be faithful in your attendance and in your participation in group functions. Get to know the people.

◆ Invite others to join you for lunch or after-church brunch.

DEVELOP GODLY FRIENDSHIPS

As you get to know people, look for areas of common interest or mutual concern. Find ways in which you can get involved in problem-solving tasks with people. It may be feeding homeless people or visiting members of your church who are homebound. It may be helping with the children's choir or joining a group that provides assistance to missionary families.

Be willing to share your life with others. Tell what the Lord has done for you and how He has helped you through difficult times in the past. Your story will be an encouragement to the person who hears it, and in turn, the individual may feel more open in sharing something of the personal journey with you.

To Have a Friend, Be a Friend

*T*he best friendships are those that take a lifetime to build and that, therefore, last a lifetime!

Friendships take time to build. They don't happen instantly. They should never be taken for granted. The best friendships are those that take a lifetime to build and that, therefore, last a lifetime!

Ask yourself today, "What kind of friend would I really like to have?" Make a list of the traits that you'd like to see in that person. Your list may include some of these characteristics:

◆ Someone to laugh with
◆ Someone to pray with
◆ Someone who really understands what I'm going through
◆ Someone I can share secrets with
◆ Someone I can trust

Once you have made your list, ask yourself a second very important question: "Am I willing to *be* this kind of friend?" Proverbs 18:24 reminds us, "A man who has friends must himself be friendly."

Are you willing to hear another person's secrets and keep them in confidence? Are you trustworthy—will your new friend be able to trust you? Are you willing to risk sharing hurts and joys? Will you be understanding of another person's failures and shortcomings and painful memories?

Are you willing to make a mistake or let another person make a mistake? Are you willing to be vulnerable?

To have a friend, you must be a friend.

Not everybody you attempt to become friends with is likely to turn into a close personal friend. Sometimes personalities just don't mesh together as you originally hope they will. Sometimes people aren't willing to take the time or make the effort that it takes for a deep friendship to develop. Sometimes there just isn't a mutuality of interests, concerns, or backgrounds. However, unless you take some risks and make some attempts at forging a friendship, you'll never know who might become a friend and who won't!

Ask God to give you the courage to take the risk of being open and vulnerable toward another person. Usually, if you are open and willing to communicate with another person, and if you are willing to share your emotions and opinions, that person will be open and willing to communicate with you.

If You Have Lost a Friend

Not all relationships, of course, turn into true friendships or become lifelong friendships. Dear friends sometimes move away or die. At such times, it's natural and normal to feel loneliness. Don't let the loss of a friend, however, keep you from developing new friendships or strengthening your other relationships. Trust God to be the God of your friendships.

Romans 8:28 tells us that "all things work together for good to those who love God, to those who are the called according to His purpose." God is the engineer of social relationships. He has a way of bringing the right people into your life at the right times for the right purposes. Sometimes the relationships last a lifetime. Sometimes they are intended only for a season in life.

If you have lost a friend, go to the Lord and tell Him how you feel: "Lord, You know how satisfying and uplifting that relationship was to me. For some reason, You've chosen to move this person out of my life, and I'm trusting You to move someone else into my life. Help me to see that You are working for the ultimate good in both lives. Help me to find ways of giving to the new friend that You bring into my life. Give me a sense of joy and anticipation at what You are about to do in my life or in the life of someone else who is about to become my friend."

YOUR DEPENDENCY MUST REMAIN ON THE LORD

The Lord may send someone into your life who will satisfy your longing to be with another person—as a friend, a confidant, or a spouse. That person must always be seen as an extension of God's presence, not as a replacement for it.

We must never become so dependent on others that we rely on them emotionally to satisfy our needs, to meet our desires, or to fulfill us completely. In the first place, no person can truly do that, no matter how wonderful or how loving the person is. No person can completely fulfill or satisfy another person's need for togetherness or oneness. It simply isn't possible. When we anticipate that, we are setting up a false expectation, and in so doing, we are setting ourselves up for great disappointment.

Too often, someone who expects another to provide complete fulfillment clings, begs, cajoles, nags, or continually cries out for attention and affection from that friend or spouse. The heart's cries often push away the other person rather than attract the person. And when the other person moves away emotionally—or in some cases, physically—the person who is crying out for intimacy feels rejected once again. The cycle continues, with ever increasing loneliness and feelings of isolation.

God desires to break that cycle. He is the only One who can truly satisfy the heart's desire for wholeness and together-ness. The desire we feel is actually and ultimately a desire to be one with Him. And He alone knows how to bring that oneness about in our lives.

Once we recognize this and turn to God to satisfy our loneliness, we are in a healthier position to receive the love and affection of persons God sends into our lives. Rather than lean on them and become emotionally dependent on them for our meaning in life, we are able to contribute to their lives and be involved in a healthy, loving, give-and-receive relationship with them.

If someone begins to trust in another person to the extent that the trust is in that person rather than in God, the relationship will eventually self-destruct; it will collapse. God is a jealous God. He wants a relationship with His children, and when He finds that one person is relying on another human being to do what only He can do, He often finds a way to end that relationship.

You must never trust another person to provide every-thing you need. No human being is capable of giving to another human being everything that is required for life be-cause life is made up of more than material things. Much of life is made up of immaterial things, spiritual things. For that reason, only God can provide everything you need to live a peaceful, joyful, fulfilling life.

You must never trust another person to deliver you from evil or to protect you from evil's power. Only God can truly deliver you from the power of the enemy in your life, and only He can tear down the strongholds that hold you captive. Only God can be the impenetrable shield for the assaults of the devil against you.

A friend who seeks to be a substitute for God is no friend! A true friend will point you to God and help you build a relationship with God.

A true friend will not allow you to become dependent. A true friend will encourage you to rely on God for your emotional strength. On whom do you rely for your emotional strength? On whom do you draw in gaining approval? On whose opinion do you rely in making decisions and taking action related to your personal problems, responsibilities, and opportunities? If you rely on another human being, you are dependent on that human being. If you rely on God, you are dependent on God. You cannot be dependent on both at the same time.

What happens, however, is that as we depend on God to be the Source of emotional security, strength, and ability, He allows us to develop relationships with others in which we are truly interdependent. We have something to give to a relationship—something we have received from the Lord. In turn, we are able to receive from others without sapping them or draining them because we are not relying on them totally for our identity. The interdependent relationship—a true giving-and-

A friend who seeks to be a substitute for God is no friend! A true friend will point you to God and help you build a relationship with God.

✳

receiving relationship—is a healthy one. No one person loses. Rather, both win!

If you don't invite the Lord to become the One on whom you depend, you cannot truly engage in a giving-and-receiving relationship with others. The relationship is more likely a tug-of-war, and very often, one person becomes a continual tugger and the other becomes more and more a resister. If you continue to cling to a person who is feeling emotionally burdened by your dependency, that person is likely to withdraw from you, and you will feel an even greater need to cling. The more you attempt to draw close and to wrap yourself around that person, the more the person will pull away. A vicious and unhealthy cycle starts that ultimately brings a great deal of pain to both parties.

CLAIM YOUR DELIVERANCE

I have found it extremely beneficial on a number of occasions to claim I John 5:14–15 as a reality in my life. These verses say, "Now this is the confidence that we have in Him, that if we ask anything according to His will, He hears us. And if we know that He hears us, whatever we ask, we know that we have the petitions that we have asked of Him."

What do you desire from the Lord? Is it in line with God's Word? Does it match up with what the Bible teaches? Is it a promise of God to you? Is it something that you know God desires for you to have?

Then state that desire with boldness, and say to the

Lord, "I am standing on this Scripture and believing that what I desire, I now have in Jesus' name."

For example, if you are struggling today with loneliness, you can rest assured that God doesn't desire for you to be lonely. He desires for you to have friends, to be a friend, and above all, to know Him as your Friend of friends. You can say with confidence, "Lord, I know that You don't want me to be lonely. I have a desire to be freed from loneliness. I claim Your Word today as applying to me. I believe that You will be the total and complete satisfaction for loneliness in my life. I trust You to fill the void that I feel. I trust You to provide for me the friends on this earth who are good, right, and pleasing in Your sight."

The Lord invites you to cling to Him. You can never sap Him dry or cause His emotional strength to be diminished. He says to you, "Lean on Me."

It is only the Lord who never pulls away from a relationship, who never backs out, who never gives up on a person, who never is drained, who always has more to give, and who invites more dependency.

When you trust in the Lord to be the Source of your joy and your deep need for companionship, you'll find that you have more to give to others. You will share, not sap. You will build up, not drain. You will uplift, not overburden. The relationship will be a healthy one, not a draining or destructive one. It will be a true friendship. And true friendship banishes loneliness.

TRUTH CAPSULE

When you are feeling lonely . . .

1. Turn first to the Lord. He would love to spend time with you! Talk to Him about how you are feeling. Ask Him to comfort your heart, and to send a friend your way.
2. Call a friend. If you don't have a close Christian friend you can call, seek to make such a friend.

My excess baggage from loneliness.

_____
_____
_____
_____
_____
_____
_____
_____
_____

How I can lighten this load.

_____
_____
_____
_____
_____
_____
_____
_____

God is the source of my strength.

*Words
of
comfort
and
healing
to
those
who
are*

FEARFUL

2

The early years of my life were tumultuous. I never knew what was coming next, and I had no confidence that I could count on tomorrow—either that it would exist, or that it would be the same as the day I was living. I certainly had no confidence that tomorrow would be brighter.

My insecurities and fears as a child were no doubt rooted in four basic facts of my life back then.

The message I received said, "Don't take any risks. Life is scary, and you're going to get hurt." ◆

First, we moved seventeen times in the first sixteen years of my life. I never knew where we might be living next.

Second, we never really seemed to have enough—especially in the early years. My mother was struggling as a single parent, and most of the time, it was all she could do to keep dinner on the table and a roof over our heads.

I remember answering the door on more than one occasion to find the insurance man standing there, ready to collect his weekly premium payment, and my mother hid behind the door insisting that I tell him that she wasn't at home.

Even though we were poor, my mother always made sure I had a clean pair of bib overalls. We were never dirty. And even in our poverty, my mother was always quick to share what we did have with others—even if just a scrap of bread.

The third reason for my early insecurities and fears probably lay in the fact that my mother bore the sole responsibility for an active, curious son. She frequently said to me, "Don't walk in the street." "Watch out." "Be careful." "Don't fall down." "Don't hurt yourself." Her message of caution, however, was one that I internalized as doom and gloom. The message I received said, "Don't take any risks. Life is scary, and you're going to get hurt."

The fourth reason for my insecurities and fears as a child was far more insidious than the other three. I was raised with a concept that God was a stern judge, just waiting to pounce on a little boy who might step out of line. In my early childhood, the thought never dawned on me to do anything really bad. I was too scared!

All of these factors resulted in my arriving at adulthood with several ideas deeply ingrained in me:

◆ Don't put down roots very deeply. You could be pulled up at any minute.

◆ Don't squander what you have. You may not be able to replace it.

◆ Don't take risks.

◆ Don't fail God.

Taken as a whole, this outlook on life is one of deep emotional insecurity, anxiety, and fear.

Again, I know that I'm not alone in my experience with these emotions. Everywhere we look today, we find people living anxious lives. Our anxieties penetrate every aspect of who we are and what we do.

Our leaders are anxious about the economy, the world's hot spots of war, and their own political futures.

Parents are anxious about their children and about how they are going to pay their bills, hold their marriages together, and keep their jobs.

Children are anxious about school, their futures, the opinions of their friends, and in too many cases, the stability of their family.

If we had one word to describe our society it might just be *anxious*. Anxious people say things such as:

"I don't know what I can count on anymore. The whole world seems to be changing faster than I can take it all in."

"I never know if my wife will be home when I get there. My children have the same question mark hanging over their heads every day when they come home from school."

"My husband comes and goes as he likes. I never really know what kind of mood he'll be in or if he'll be drunk and abusive. I feel like I'm walking on eggshells most of the time."

Pastors and counselors hear statements like these nearly every day.

*I*f we had one word to describe our society it might just be *anxious.*

THE ROOT OF ANXIETY

Anxiety is fear of the future. We feel anxious when tomorrow looks grim, when the future holds no promise of change, when our lives spin out of control and we aren't sure what's going to happen from one moment to the next.

Sometimes a person imagines or perceives a failure even before he makes an effort. He sees no way he can win, succeed, or come out of an impending crisis unscathed.

✳

Sometimes anxiety is rooted in a person's feelings that he is incapable of handling a new challenge. He imagines or perceives a failure even before he makes an effort. He sees no way he can win, succeed, or come out of an impending crisis unscathed.

Sometimes anxiety is rooted in a person's setting standards that are too high. She constantly measures herself against a perceived goal or standard that is virtually impossible for her—and perhaps for anyone—to reach.

Sometimes anxiety is rooted in a person's feeling torn between two opinions or between two people he loves. For example, a person may find himself in between a parent and a spouse, a child may feel as if he is in a tug-of-war between two parents, or an employee may feel caught in a conflict between his boss and his peers.

Sometimes anxiety is rooted in unresolved hostility over a past issue. The person continues to live in a perceived reality of past hatred, anger, or bitterness that may not actually exist in the present.

Very often our anxieties manifest themselves in relationship to the very basic things of life: what we wear, what we eat, and where we live. We become anxious that we aren't making a good appearance. We become anxious that we won't have another meal to eat or that we won't be able to pay next month's mortgage. We become anxious that we aren't earning enough money, saving enough for retirement, or getting ahead as fast as we should be.

Jesus knew all about these causes of anxiety. Anxiety over life's basic needs was a problem when He walked the earth. He taught His disciples,

Therefore I say to you, do not worry about your life, what you will eat; nor about the body, what you will put on. Life is more than food, and the body is more than clothing. Consider the ravens, for they neither sow nor reap, which have neither storehouse nor barn; and God feeds them. Of how much more value are you than the birds? And which of you by worrying can add one cubit to his stature? If you then are not able to do the least, why are you anxious for the rest? Consider the lilies, how they grow: they neither toil nor spin; and yet I say to you, even Solomon in all his glory was not arrayed like one of these. If then God so clothes the grass, which today is in the field and tomorrow is thrown into the oven, how much more will He clothe you, O you of little faith? And do not seek what you should eat or what you should drink, nor have an anxious mind. For all these things the nations of the world seek after, and your Father knows that you need these things (Luke 12:22–30).

Anxiety manifests itself in several ways:

◆ Increased irritability

◆ A continual vacillation of opinion

◆ Repeated errors of judgment

◆ Feelings of persecution, even if no persecutor can be identified

◆ Procrastination

◆ Increased use of chemicals as a means of escape from pain, sleeplessness, or nervous tension

◆ Low productivity

On one occasion Jesus referred to anxieties as "the cares of this world," and He said that they "choke the word" so that a person becomes unfruitful (Matt. 13:22). Anxiety nearly always results in a person's becoming less productive. In fact, the greater the anxiety a person feels, the less productive the person tends to become. The same holds true for spiritual productivity, or the bearing of spiritual fruit. The person who is bound up with insecurities, anxieties, and fears cannot be truly fruitful in the kingdom of God.

HOW ARE YOU TO OVERCOME ANXIETY?

To overcome anxiety, you must deal with your overwhelming fear of the future. You need something that can anchor your life so that no matter what happens, you won't be blown off course. The only thing that can anchor you is God, and the only way you discover who He is, is through Jesus Christ. Ultimately, if you will build your relationship with Him, God will enable you to face whatever is happening in your life and to come out victoriously. You may go through difficulty, hardship, or trial—but as long as you are anchored to Him, you will have hope.

The first and primary step, then, to overcome anxiety is to make sure that you have a personal relationship with Jesus Christ. To do that, you need to come sincerely and honestly to God and to say, "I want to have a relationship with You. I accept what You have done for me—that You have sent Jesus

Christ to this earth to die in my place and to be the sacrifice for my sins. I accept that You desire to have a relationship with me. I receive today the free gift of Your grace that You have made available to me. I choose to follow the Lord."

If you have never trusted Jesus as your Savior, the biggest problem in your life is a sin problem—a problem of unbelief. That's at the root of anxiety. When we don't trust God with our future, we have no one to trust. The result is fear. You cannot be truly secure about any other thing in life until you are secure in your relationship with the Lord.

Nothing but Jesus will calm your anxiety. You may look at other issues and blame other people, but the fact is, until Jesus is a part of your life, you will always fear the unknown.

There's a part of you that God made for Himself. Nothing can fill that void or occupy that part of you except Him. As long as you remain apart from God and refuse to allow Jesus Christ to fill that part of yourself with Himself, you will feel that something is missing. And that feeling of something missing, something wrong, something not right, or something not whole is the feeling of insecurity.

Part of your security in accepting Jesus into your life as your Savior is the promise Jesus makes to you that He will never abandon you. He will never leave you. Jesus promised, "I'll never leave you nor forsake you."

We may move away from God, but He never moves away from us. We may reject Jesus, but He never rejects us. That's why He is our anchor.

SEEK HIS KINGDOM

Once you have established a relationship with Jesus, your Surety and your Security, you must take a second step. Jesus spoke of this step as He concluded His discourse on the ravens and the lilies: "But seek the kingdom of God, and all these things shall be added to you" (Luke 12:31).

The way to get to know Jesus so that you can truly come to count on Him is to seek the kingdom of God—in other words, to know how God's kingdom operates. What does God require? What does God desire? How does God want us to live with Him and in relationship with one another?

You get answers to these questions by reading God's Word. Begin by reading the Gospels, especially the gospel of John. Get to know who Jesus is. Meet Him! Encounter Him! Get to know His character, His words, His reactions, His heartbeat toward men and women, including you.

And then read the Psalms. You'll encounter the feelings of David, who experienced many hardships and struggles and who felt the way we often feel today. You'll discover that you are not alone in what you are feeling, and that God can and will meet you where you are.

As you begin to read the Word of God and absorb it into your life, the Spirit of God moves to drive out your fears. The process is a fairly straightforward one:

◆ The more you focus on who God is and what God is like, the more your attitude and your thinking will begin to change. You will begin to line them up with the truth of

God's Word. You will begin to feel and think the way God feels and thinks.

◆ As you begin to feel and think like God feels and thinks, fears fall away. A sense of confidence and assurance builds. You will find yourself relying upon and trusting God more and more.

◆ The more you put your trust in God, the more you discover that He never lets you down. You can count on Him! When that happens, a boldness develops in your spirit so that anxiety is a thing of the past. You know who you are in Christ and who Christ is in you! You come to the place where you trust Him to be with you and to help you through whatever circumstance or experience life hands you.

Above all, you will discover that God is your ally. He is not your enemy or a stern demanding judge waiting to pounce on your every error. He loves you, and He desires that you always grow in your relationship with Him.

God is your ally. He is not your enemy or a stern demanding judge waiting to pounce on your every error.

Are You Afraid of God?

Some people struggle with being afraid of God. Their fears are fears about God, not about people or situations.

I frequently say to people who tell me they are scared of God, "Tell me about your relationship with your father."

To children, the person most like a god to them is the father. The father in the home is the ultimate authority. He has power and control over their lives unlike any person other than God. If children grow up afraid of the earthly father, it is very easy for that fear to be transferred to God.

The difference is that a human father is human—and as

a human being, he couldn't help making mistakes. He may have mistreated you, neglected you, or been insensitive to you. But our heavenly Father is a God of love, forgiveness, goodness, mercy, graciousness, and kindness—a Father who always wants the best for His children.

We need to ask ourselves, "What is God really like?" Not what we may have been taught He is like or what we may have supposed He is like based on our experience with an earthly father—but what He is really like.

The best way to find out what the Father is like is to look at Jesus. Jesus said that He was the mirror image of God. He didn't do anything that the Father didn't do. Everything He did was what the Father did. Jesus treated people with the utmost kindness, respect, and generosity.

Take Zacchaeus, for example. He was one of the lowest of the low in Jewish circles. He was not only a tax collector on the side of the oppressor, Rome, but he was dishonest in his dealings with people. Jesus didn't say to him, "You're a scoundrel, Zacchaeus. I'm coming after you with both barrels blazing." No! Jesus said to Zacchaeus, "Come on down out of that tree. I'm going home with you for lunch." (See Luke 19:1–10.)

Then there was the woman at the well. She was a notorious woman in her city. She had been married five times and was presently living with a man to whom she wasn't married. Jesus didn't say to her, "You're a sinner. Don't talk to Me." Instead, Jesus said to her, "If you really want to find true satisfaction in your life, turn to Me as the Well of your life. I'll give you living water that is lasting." (See John 4:5–41.)

And what about the woman who had been caught in the

act of adultery? According to the law, she was to be stoned to death. Did Jesus condemn her? No! He said, "Go your way and don't do what you've been doing anymore." (See John 8:3–11.)

Again and again in the Gospels we see Jesus moving toward people, healing people, comforting people, raising the dead, restoring people, delivering people from the power of the devil, and blessing people. His nature was to cry when His friends cried, to laugh when His friends laughed, and to forgive their sins so that their tears might turn to joy! And thus is the character of God.

God is just, but because God is also a God of mercy, His judgments about us as His children are for our good.

God is all-powerful, but because God is also a God of love, His power moves heaven and earth so that we might experience all of the good things He has for us.

Facing the Crisis Moment of Fear

As you face a particularly fearful moment—for example, it may be a conversation that you know you need to have with a spouse or child, or the fact that you need to walk out to your car in a dark parking lot late at night—do two things.

First, ask God for His wisdom in that moment—for just that precise circumstance or situation. Ask Him to show you what to do or to reveal to you what you are to say. If you don't have the calm inner assurance that He is directing you and is present with you, don't make a move. Listen in your heart for His guidance. The Spirit of God may remind you of a verse of Scripture that will give you confidence. He may bring to your mind an idea that you hadn't thought of before. He may prompt you to call a friend to pray with you or for you, or to go with you into the difficult situation. He may reveal to you a better way to handle the encounter—for example, to have another person present for the conversation or to have a security guard walk with you to your car.

Jesus referred to the Spirit of God as the "Spirit of truth" (John 15:26). He won't lead you into error or danger. He will always lead you and guide you into the truth of a situation or to the heart of a matter. He will always lead you into what is life-giving and life-sustaining. If any idea comes into your mind that involves something contrary to God's Word—that prompts you to sin or to do anything against the teachings of Jesus—you can be assured that the idea is not from the Spirit of truth.

Second, remind yourself of God's promises to you. Say aloud to yourself, "Lord, You said that You would never leave me nor forsake me. I'm trusting You to be with me now!"

If you haven't read God's Word, and if you haven't read it sufficiently to have it embedded in your heart and memory, the Spirit of God won't be able to quicken that Word in you or to bring God's Word to your mind. You must first know God's Word before you can be reminded of it. That's all the more reason to turn to God's Word daily and to build a foundation of trust in God based on what God said He would be and do for you.

MAKE A DECISION TO TURN OFF THE
OLD TAPES

Beyond having a relationship with Jesus and seeking God's kingdom by reading His Word and learning about who He is and what He desires and requires of us, we must take responsibility for turning off the old tapes—erasing or replacing the message on the tape of memory.

One day I was facing a situation that called for some personal risk, and I heard my mother's voice begin to speak to me or, rather, to the little boy inside me, "Don't try it. It's dangerous. You'll get hurt."

I thought, *Why, that's just like a tape going off in my head. I'm not even really thinking those thoughts about this situation. I'm just replaying what I've heard since I was a little boy: "Don't take risks; don't walk out into the street; don't try anything scary."* I decided that was enough of that! Life may have difficult moments, but the Bible tells me that I can do all things through Christ Jesus. (See Phil. 4:13.)

I don't know what tapes you might be listening to today, but I am nearly 100 percent positive that you have mental tapes and that you are listening to them.

It may be the tape that says, "I've got to polish the floor today in case the pastor comes by to visit," or "I can't give this amount of money because I may not have enough to pay the bills," or "I'd better not open my mouth because I may look stupid."

It's time to take action against the tapes from our past. They are rooted in anxiety and fear. If you hear a message begin to play in your head and it causes you to trust God less or fear God more, make a decision by your will, "I'll not have any more of that!"

MAKE A DECISION TO TRUST GOD COMPLETELY

Shortly after I was saved as a young teenager, I discovered that I had two great desires. One was to read the Bible, and the other was to obey God. I felt the person in my life who knew the most about obeying God was my grandfather.

When I was sixteen, I went to see him for a week. All I wanted to do was talk to him and have him talk to me. He was about seventy years old at the time, retired from preaching but still doing a little bit of farming in his backyard at the edge of town.

My grandfather talked to me all week. I remember feeling overwhelmed by him and what he said. His words had a profound effect on my life.

One of the things my grandfather said was, "Charles, if God tells you to run your head through a brick wall, you head for the wall, and when you get there, God will make a hole for it." That was my grandfather's way of saying "Obey God."

My grandfather also told me about when God called him to preach. He had been in the Methodist church at the time and they threw him out because he claimed to have entire sanctification. He was walking home one night and was struggling about whether it was really God who was calling him to preach. He didn't have a great deal of formal education, and he could barely read his Bible. He said, "I got down on my knees on that dirt road and said, 'God, if You're the One who really wants me to preach, let me see two stars fall.' " He looked up and sure enough, he saw two falling stars at precisely that moment. I interpreted what my grandfather said in this way: "God will move heaven and earth to show you His will for your life if you really want to do His will."

After my grandfather started to preach, he decided to buy a tent and begin preaching in it. The tent cost three hundred dollars, and he had no idea how he was going to get that much money. He had a vision while he was praying, and he saw a little house with a fence around it. He recognized it in his vision as a place he thought he had seen one time during a visit to a little town not very far away.

The next day he went into that town and walked up and down the streets until he found the house he had seen in his vision. At that point, he got scared. Still, he knew that God had something to do with it, so he finally got up his courage and knocked on the door. A woman answered and said, "Why, Mr. Stanley, I've been wanting to talk to you." She invited him in, and after they had talked for a few minutes, she excused herself and said, "I've got something for you." She came back in the room and handed him a brown paper bag. In it were three hundred one-dollar bills. She said, "God told me to give this to you." I thought about that later and put that experience into these words: *You trust Me, and I'll provide all your needs. Don't look to anybody else. Look to Me.*

I also remember my grandfather telling me during my visit about an incident that happened to him while he was preaching. Two inebriated men came in one Sunday morning and sat down on the right side of the church. They started

God will move heaven and earth to reveal His will to you if you really want to know it and do it.

making a noise during the service so my grandfather stopped his sermon and said, "You either shut up or get out." They got up and walked out.

After the service, nearly everybody had left the church when two deacons came rushing up to my grandfather and said, "Those two fellows are outside, and they have butcher knives. They're planning to kill you. We're going to call the police." He said, "No, I don't want you to call the police." They insisted. He did, too: "No, I don't want you to call the police. I want you to go home." The deacons finally left.

My grandfather took his old brown Thompson Chain-Reference® Bible and knelt down at the altar with it and said, "God, I'm preaching for You and I'm trusting You." Then he got up and walked out the front door of the church. Sure enough, the two fellows were at the bottom of the steps, but my grandfather just walked down the steps between the two of them—the smell of alcohol strong. The two men froze in their tracks.

Grandfather walked home. While he was eating Sunday lunch with the family, he heard sirens. That was a fairly unusual sound in their small town so they all got up and rushed toward the sound of the sirens a couple of blocks away. Those same two men had driven their car into a light pole. The car burst into flames, and they both burned to death. Later, I realized that God had used my grandfather to tell me, *Trust Me to be your protector.*

On the bus ride home after that week with my grandfather, I came to a conclusion: If God worked in my grandfather's life like that, I can trust Him to work in my life.

I thought about all the Old Testament characters who

had experienced God's work in their lives, and I began to read in depth about Abraham, Joseph, David, Daniel, and Moses. Those were my five favorites. I felt driven to read their stories again and again and think about how God had worked in my grandfather's life.

As I looked back, the stories my grandfather told me gave me the guiding principles of my life:

◆ Obey God and leave all the consequences to Him. Trust Him to make a way.

◆ God will move heaven and earth to reveal His will to you if you really want to know it and do it.

◆ God will provide all your needs.

◆ God will protect you.

Each principle has to do with trust. We must ask ourselves periodically, "Am I really trusting God? Am I willing to put all of my cares and concerns into His hands and let Him deal with them and with me?"

QUESTIONS TO ASK DAILY

There are four questions we are wise to ask ourselves on a daily basis.

Question #1: "Am I trusting God today to provide my daily needs?"

God's Word says, "God shall supply all your need according to His riches in glory by Christ Jesus" (Phil. 4:19).

We have the privilege of coming to God with every need

we have. God is our all-wise, all-powerful, and all-loving heavenly Father—who loved us so much He gave His Son for our eternal salvation. We can certainly trust Him to provide for the things we need to live from day to day on this earth.

Remind yourself of Jesus' words in Luke 12:30 after He had described how God takes care of the ravens and the lilies: "Your Father knows that you need these things."

It is God's responsibility to provide the things we need. It is our responsibility to trust Him and to keep our focus on who He is and what He supplies rather than on what is missing or lacking in our lives. Too often, we shift our focus so that it is exactly the opposite of God's plan. We start trusting in what we have and looking at what we don't have and blaming God for our lack! Rather, let's trust God to be the Source of our total supply and keep our eyes on what He provides.

Why am I so assured that God will supply your need? Because it is His character to be *faithful.* God's nature doesn't change. He is always the same.

At two points in my early life, I experienced God's provision in profound ways.

When I was thirteen, I got a newspaper route to deliver the *Commercial Appeal* on Monday and Thursday mornings. That job gave me my first real spending money. It was God's provision to me through *work*—and I was not only grateful for it, but I did my utmost to do the best job possible. The newspaper had contests for the delivery boys—for example, a contest to see who could get the most new customers and a contest to see who received the fewest complaints. I made it a point to win as many of those contests as I possibly could.

Eventually, I was able to secure a newspaper route that required me to deliver papers in the mornings and then again in the afternoons.

At that point, I was in tall cotton. I was making about $18 a week—enough to buy the things I needed, including suits and shoes for church. My mother always insisted that I had a good suit and a good pair of shoes to wear to church, so I'd put a dollar down and then pay on a suit until I had paid for it. Average suits in those days cost $29.95—a really nice one went for $34.95. About twice a year, Charles Stanley, paperboy, bought a new suit for himself. Did God provide it? Yes. Through an opportunity to work.

As you are trusting the Lord to be the Source of your provision, look for ways in which He gives you opportunities to work. Be sensitive to ideas He may give you and people He brings your way.

The Lord also provided for me in my teen years in a miraculous way—a way that was totally through His doing, with no effort on my part.

I was standing on the street corner one night, talking to a friend, and I was telling him that I believed the Lord was calling me to preach. I said, "You know, I've got to go to school, and I don't have any money." I didn't know him all that well. We were just talking about our lives in a rather casual way. I was delivering newspapers but after I paid for my basic needs in life, there wasn't a lot left over to save for school.

At that moment in our conversation, the pastor of my church walked by, and Julian said, "Mr. Hammock, Charles believes the Lord has called him to preach. Do you think you can help him go to school?"

Pastor Hammock said, "Well, I might. Why don't you come by and see me?"

So I went to his office one day, and it turned out to be one of the most important afternoons of my life. Pastor Hammock arranged for me to receive a four-year full scholarship to the University of Richmond, about 150 miles north of Danville.

I left for college with seventy-five dollars to my name, and I graduated four years later not owing anybody anything but gratitude. One time I was down to having ten cents in my pocket, but I never was completely without money. I worked, of course, during the summer months, but I never had to worry about tuition or room and board.

Did God provide for me? Yes. He used *generous, giving people* to bring a miracle of provision into my life.

Whether through opportunities to work, or through the generosity of others, God not only can, but will, make His provision available to you. You can trust Him to do it!

Question #2: "Am I trusting You, God, to be my security today?"

We must keep our eyes on God, not on the world situation, the stock market, the bond market, the current prime interest rates, or any other thing.

Believe me, if you get your eyes off God and onto what's happening in the world, you'll find plenty to be insecure and anxious about! You can pick up any newspaper today and turn on any nightly newscast, and then turn to your Bible and conclude, "Well, it's happening just the way the Bible said it would!" The world is in upheaval. The painful birth pangs of the end seem to be coming faster and faster. Even though times may be changing, mores may be shifting, political nations may be rising and falling, you can have security in knowing that you are anchored to an unchanging God, the Sovereign of this universe. He knows the human heart. He allows human wickedness to express itself to a degree, but only to a degree. He ultimately is in control.

No matter what is happening in the world, we can trust God to guide us and to help us make the right decisions in our relationships, our finances, and our vocations. We can't change the world, but we can put our trust in God who is in control of this world and who can change our lives to conform to His plan for us. We can walk through even the most difficult times with an awesome sense of inner quietness and assurance that the God who is in control of the world is also in control of our lives. We can trust Him also to use various circumstances to grow us up in our faith and to strengthen us.

You can have more policies, bond coupons, and savings accounts than you can count and still lose everything. Or you may die before you have an opportunity to cash in any of them. Ultimately, the only security is your relationship with the Lord.

Now, in a very practical way, we can trust God to manifest His security for us and to lead us into the very methods and means that will provide daily financial security for us. We do this by asking God about every decision related to our lives.

If someone approaches you about increasing an insurance policy, talk to God about it before you make a decision. Ask Him, "Is this something You want me to do?" It may be that He will say, *No, I have something better down the line for you,* or *Not now. I want you to trust Me for your future in another way.* It may be that God will say in your heart, *Yes, this is something I want you to have. I have led this person into your life so that you will have what you need later.*

The issue may be one of property. Ask the Lord before you make an investment, "Is this something You want me to have? Is this a wise purchase to make?" Listen for His guidance. Watch for ways in which He will confirm His will to you.

God will never lead you to make an unwise decision. Again, His very character is *wisdom.* He will not go against His nature in leading you.

It is sad that countless people around the world are turning to the occult to provide security for them. They believe that in knowing the future—through visits to mediums and fortune-tellers and readers of tea leaves and tarot cards—they will be able to manipulate the future. They don't realize that they are turning to those who are in association with the father of lies—the devil himself—in order to get truth! Why would anyone want to turn to a convicted liar to get truth?

And what kind of future do these fortune-tellers see? Many times those who seek to know the future come away with a supposed insight into a future that is truly frightening. They "see" things that cause them to take rash actions, which are often very destructive to them or to others.

Furthermore, fortune-tellers provide no help with the future they tell. They cannot help a person prepare for the future or cope with it.

The person who begins to trust in a fortune-teller—someone working off the power of the devil—is actually putting trust in the devil and developing a relationship with the enemy of the soul. That relationship will turn out to be extremely unsettling and ultimately destructive.

People who deal in the occult are not the only ones who can claim to tell you what your future holds. Many well-meaning people may try to tell you what to do or how to respond to today's troubles so that you can have a positive future.

Never depend on another person to tell you what your future holds or to define your future for you. No person knows fully what is best for you, what is right for you, or what God has planned for your good in the future. God alone knows that—not a teacher, not a pastor, not a mentor, not a spiritual director, not a parent, not a friend. Only God knows what He has ordained for your good in the days ahead. He alone sees how bright your future can be in Him.

A wise counselor may help you discern God's plan for you. A counselor may help you explore the ways in which God is revealing His plan to you. A counselor may be able to help you see things about yourself and God's plan that you haven't been able to see. But that is a far cry from dictating your future or saying with certainty, "This is the way things will be for you."

Only God knows with certainty what tomorrow holds. He reveals the future when it is to our benefit to know it. He says in His Word, "I will instruct you and teach you in the way you should go;/ I will guide you with My eye" (Ps. 32:8). For God to guide us with His eye, we need to be focused on Him!

We all know what it means to take a cue from someone by the look given to us—to turn in one direction or another, to stop, to start, or to put our attention on something in particular. To get that direction, however, we need to look the person squarely in the eye. The same holds true for the guidance we receive from God. He can't guide us with His eye if we look at someone or something other than Him. He said,

> Trust in the LORD with all your heart,
> And lean not on your own understanding;
> In all your ways acknowledge Him,
> And He shall direct your paths (Prov. 3:5–6).

God makes numerous promises in His Word to direct us, guide us, and lead us step-by-step into the future He has prepared for us. God is infinite in His wisdom. He is also infinite in His love for us. He is going to reveal to us only what is the most loving thing for us to know.

Question #3: "Am I willing to risk some of what I have today because I am trusting God to meet my needs tomorrow?"

My mother was a great giver. She never threw away a crust of bread. If she saw a hungry child, she always did her best to give him something to eat.

I have met many people who lived during the days of the Great Depression, however, who even today feel a need to keep their cupboards full. In many of these cases, the person is trusting in a full cupboard for tomorrow's provision rather than trusting in the Lord.

We need to ask ourselves, "Are we trusting in our fullness, or are we trusting in God?"

Our fullness may be a full bank account or a full portfolio of stocks or a full retirement account or a full Social Security check.

God doesn't care how much is in your financial cupboard. He knows that He is going to provide your next meal for you whether there's an abundance in your pocketbook or not! The real question is, how much trust is in your heart?

Can you really trust God to provide for your next meal? Your next payment? Your next utility bill? Your next repair?

There are those who have full cupboards and absolutely no joy or peace in their hearts. As much as they have, they have no real inner sense of security. On the other hand, there are those who have nearly empty cupboards and yet are filled with joy, peace, and confidence. The issue is not a matter of what we have or don't have; it's a matter of how much we are trusting God.

My grandfather said, "You look to God as your Source. We're all just channels. He's the Source. If you look to people, you'll get dependent on them. If you look to God, He'll handle the people."

I took my grandfather at his word because I knew that in so doing, I was also taking the Lord at His Word.

*Y*ou won't
need to
compute,
figure,
calculate,
manipulate, or
connive to get
what the Lord
desires for you
to have in the
future. He
already knows
what you
need.

✳

In all my years in the ministry, I've asked only one person for money. We were installing an 800 number for our television and radio ministry at the time. I was on the phone one day with a man, and I found myself telling him about the new project in the course of our conversation. He asked me how much it was going to cost. I said, "About $250,000," and then I added as an afterthought, "Say, why don't you give us $25,000?" He said, "You've got it."

In retrospect, I've often wondered if I should have asked for more! Still, there was nothing calculated or manipulative about my asking. It was as innocent a question as the one my friend Julian asked Pastor Hammock. In both cases, God had a generous person in the right place at the right time to meet a need.

You won't need to compute, figure, calculate, manipulate, or connive to get what the Lord desires for you to have in the future. He already knows what you need, and He is already arranging people and circumstances to be ready and available for you at just the right time.

Question #4: "Am I trusting You today, Lord, to show me Your way?"

Part of trusting God with the future is trusting Him to show you which decisions to make and when to take action on them. You can ask the Lord to show you what to do and when to do it, and to give you confirmation that you are on the right track.

When I was a senior in college, I went through a real struggle. I took ROTC, and while playing on an intramural air force football team, I fell and tore a ligament in my leg. I was put into a heavy cast, which I had to wear for several weeks.

The week that the cast came off was exam week. I scored a 50 on my trigonometry test and a 70 on a history test (which was my major). In all, I failed every test but one that week, and I could hardly afford a D in my major!

I felt a tremendous burden. I got out my Bible and read it to God. I even got out my hymnal and read it to Him. I kept crying out to God, "God, I could fail to graduate here at the very end!" No answer came from heaven. It was a terrible week.

On Thursday night of that week, I went down to Thomas Hall, and as I walked there, I began to cry. I stopped and looked up toward heaven, and I said, "God, I have no business asking You this, but I've really got to know what is going on. Are You there? Am I on the right road?" Then I remembered my grandfather's story, and I added, "If I am on the right road, will You please let me see two stars fall?"

I stared up into a clear night sky, the Milky Way splashed across it so brightly. There were tons of lights in the sky that could have fallen that night. But as I watched, not one star fell.

I went to the room of two friends and said, "I need you to pray for me." They prayed for me until two o'clock in the morning when I returned to my dorm room. God hadn't spoken.

On Saturday evening, my friend Avery came by and said, "Let's go get a hamburger." Our college didn't serve meals on Saturday nights, so we headed for town. On the way back to the dorm, he said, "Let me show you a shortcut," and we walked across the back of an Episcopal churchyard. He stopped and said, "Isn't it a beautiful night?" We looked up at the sky, and at that moment, two stars fell simultaneously at what seemed to be only inches apart.

I went to my room, and as I was brushing my teeth, I heard the Lord say in my heart, *Remember what you asked of Me?*

I said, "Oh, that's happened a thousand times before. I've seen lots of falling stars."

He said, *But have you ever seen two of them fall at the same time?*
"No."

Have you ever seen them fall as you were standing in the yard of a church?

"No."

Had you ever asked Me before?
"No."

I went back to my desk and tried to study—to no avail. Finally, I knelt down beside my bed. God settled my call into the ministry that night . . . forever. I said to the Lord, "Whatever You've got for me, I'm trusting You, and I'm trusting You to lead me each step of the way."

I got up off my knees that night feeling permanently anchored to God and His will for my life.

DEALING WITH GRIPPING FEAR

Many people seem to be experiencing *panic attacks* or *anxiety attacks*. When the attacks hit, the heart pounds, the skin grows clammy, and they feel weak and faint. They are truly in the grip of a sudden onslaught of fear and insecurity.

What can you do if such an attack strikes you?

The first thing you need to do is to turn your focus to God. Say aloud to Him, "Father, You are my heavenly Father. You promised to meet all my needs. You said that You are living inside me. You said that You would make me adequate for all things and in every circumstance. The apostle Paul wrote, 'I can do all things through Christ who strengthens me' (Phil. 4:13), and I'm claiming that Scripture as Your truth to me right now. I'm feeling as if I'm going to fall apart. I don't know which way to turn. I'm feeling out of control. You promised to be with me. God, I'm trusting You. I'm trusting You to be in control."

When I've experienced times of panic and I've turned to God in this way, I've discovered again and again that an awesome sense of God's quietness fills my heart. He becomes my sole focus. I see in Him a God who is full of grace and love and mercy and kindness. When I look at Him, I see One I can trust completely.

When I look at myself apart from God's presence, I see myself being *opposed*. I see the threats and accusations and negative consequences that the world holds, and my response is invariably that I feel fear. This world is a tough place. It's not something I want to try to conquer in my strength without God.

Second, you need to rebuke the fear itself in the name of Jesus. Note carefully that I said you rebuke the fear, not the person or circumstance. In dealing with the speaker of fear-causing words, or in dealing with the person who is threatening you, you need to tell the person boldly and unapologetically to be silent.

A gripping fear is not of God. The Lord does not do anything to cause us to respond with the thought or feeling, *There's nothing good about this,* or *This will destroy me.* God does not cause His people to panic or to feel as if they are losing their hold on life. As 2 Timothy 1:7 tells us, "God has not given us a spirit of fear, but of power and of love and of a sound mind." It is God's desire that we have confidence and authority over fear. We have His full permission to say, "This fear is not of God. I rebuke it in the name of Jesus!"

Several times people have stood in our church services and have begun to rattle off something that was totally opposed to God's purposes. In each instance, a spirit of fear seemed to wash over the audience as the person spoke. I've felt bold to say, "That isn't of God! I rebuke what you are saying in Jesus' name. Sit down and be quiet." I've also experienced similar incidents in my personal life. In some cases I have had to say directly to the person, "That isn't of God. I refuse to let anything of what you are saying affect me."

As a child of God, you have the authority to speak both to fear and to the one causing you to feel fear. Rebuke the fear. Demand that the speaker be quiet.

MAINTAINING THE FOCUS ON THE LORD

Although there are times when we need to rebuke the devil, he should never be our focus when tragedy, turmoil, or trauma arises.

If we focus on the devil and see him as a tyrant constantly coming at us to defeat us, we can get very fearful.

After all, the devil has a lot of famous victims in his history —from the time of Adam and Eve all the way down to the present day. Rather than give our attention to the devil and what he is trying to do *to* us, let's focus on the Lord and what He promises to do *for* us.

It's easy to wilt or to fold in the face of the devil. On the other hand, it's very difficult to fold if we turn and face God. In Him, we see our Victor, our Savior, our Deliverer, our very present Help in time of trouble!

The wonderful news is that when we turn to the Lord, we are—as the Scriptures say to do—resisting the devil. The Bible gives us the proper balance: "Submit to God. Resist the devil and he will flee from you. Draw near to God and He will draw near to you" (James 4:7–8). There's no greater resistance of the devil than to turn to God and say, "Father, I'm trusting You!"

The devil will come back around again and again, of course. That's the devil's nature. He does his best to try to tempt each person to sin for as long as that person is alive. Nobody is immune from the devil's temptations.

What can and does happen, however, is that we can become so secure in Jesus, so confident that God is our God, that the devil's temptations have less and less impact on us. We can't keep the devil from trying to do us in, but we can get to the place where we hear the devil's roar as merely a whimper.

People who work out regularly know the great benefit of resistance in exercise. Muscles are made strong through resistance against weight. The same principle holds true in the spiritual realm. The more we resist the devil by submitting ourselves to God, the stronger we become. The more we draw near to God, the less likely the devil is to seek us as easy prey.

There will be times, of course, when God may give us such complete and eternal victory over one area of sin or temptation in our lives—or over one enemy that has tormented us—that we never have to face that area of temptation or that type of torment again. That particular weakness will have been dealt with forever.

This is what happened to Moses and the children of Israel as they left Egypt. The children of Israel left without looking over their shoulders. They were given the gold and precious goods of Egypt by their former slave drivers. They had God's sign of provision and protection—the shed blood of the Passover that spared their firstborn children and livestock. And then, as if to seal their assurance that God had delivered them, the Israelites saw the chariots and horses and soldiers of Pharaoh swept away in the waters of the Red Sea, fulfilling the word of the Lord to Moses that "the Egyptians whom you see today, you shall see again no more forever" (Exod. 14:13).

In some cases, God will deliver a person from sin's bondage in a similar way.

In other cases, God will give the person a victory in a particular situation or circumstance—or a series of victories. If that is the way God seems to be working in your life, you can rest in the knowledge that God is with you, He is working in you and through you, and each time you experience a victory, you can know that God is causing your trust in Him to grow.

THE SECURITY OF HIS TOUCH

The most security that any of us have ever felt is no doubt the security felt in the enveloping arms of someone who loved us deeply—perhaps a parent, a grandparent, a spouse, a child, or a friend.

"But," you may say, "God doesn't have any arms. I can't feel His security or His touch." Oh, but you can!

It's amazing how God will send His people into our lives to touch us, hug us, hold us, and satisfy the need to experience His pure, unadulterated, genuine love. We know God's presence and feel His security, in part, through those He brings into our lives who can touch us and love us just as Jesus would if He was walking the cities where we live today.

At other times, God simply envelops us with His presence. We may cry out to Him, "Father, I have nobody but You. I need to feel You. I need to know You are there." And it's almost as if God reaches down and covers us with His presence. The psalmist described this as God covering him with His wings:

How precious is Your lovingkindness, O God!
Therefore the children of men put
    their trust under the shadow of Your wings.
They are abundantly satisfied
    with the fullness of Your house,
And You give them drink from
    the river of Your pleasures (Ps. 36:7–8).

This overwhelming sense of God's comfort can be so real that it's just as if we are being cradled in His arms, sheltered by His bosom, made safe under His everlasting wings. And indeed, we are! The feeling is one of total satisfaction, fulfillment, and security.

It is that feeling of complete security—an abiding sense of His presence with us always—that God longs for each one of us to have. It comes as we trust Him and accept from Him what He longs to give us.

EXPECT YOUR TRUST TO GROW

Trust in God—the answer to anxieties and fears—is not static.

It is not an absolute.

It is not always a constant.

It is rarely perfect or full.

Rather, it grows.

Don't be discouraged if your ability to trust God seems to wax and wane. That is only human.

The decision we must make, however, is that we are going to seek to trust God more. In times of weakness, we need to begin to trust Him. When our trust level is low, we need to trust Him more. Even in times of great trust, we must seek to trust Him *even more.*

The wonderful hope we have, of course, is that the more we trust God, the more we find God to be faithful. Thus, the more we are willing to trust, the more God shows we can trust Him.

God's nature has not changed. He is always trustworthy. What happens, rather, is that we grow in our ability to trust Him. None of us begins with a strong ability to trust. Each of us must grow into that trust. And it becomes stronger as we trust.

Finally, the stronger our trust level is in the Lord, the more our insecurities, anxieties, and fears melt away. We find ourselves able to do what Peter tells us to do, "Humble yourselves under the mighty hand of God, that He may exalt you in due time, casting all your care upon Him, for He cares for you" (1 Peter 5:6–7).

The more we humble ourselves to trust God and to rely on His hand to provide for us, protect us, and guide us, the more He builds us up in strength, faith, and wholeness. The more we cast our cares upon Him, the more He shows us how much He truly desires to care for us, give to us, and deliver us from all harm.

Are you feeling anxious or fearful today?

Run for shelter under the Lord's wings!

TRUTH CAPSULE

When you are feeling insecure, anxious, or fearful . . .

1. Reevaluate your relationship with the Lord Jesus. Are you trusting Him to be your Savior? Are you willing to follow Him as your Lord?

2. Reevaluate your commitment to reading God's Word. Are you reading it regularly? Are you drawing strength from it? Are you patterning your life after what God says to do and to be?

3. Reevaluate your willingness to trust God to provide for you, protect you, be there in your tomorrows, and make His will known to you. If you aren't trusting God to be the Source of your protection, provision, and guidance, begin to trust Him today.

4. Look for ways in which God will allow you to feel His presence—either directly or through the genuinely loving actions of others.

My excess baggage from fearfulness.

_____

_____

_____

_____

_____

_____

_____

_____

_____

How I can lighten this load.

_____

_____

_____

_____

_____

_____

_____

_____

God is the source of my strength.

Words
of
comfort
and
healing
to
those
who
are
suffering
from

3

ABUSE

*W*hen I was nine years old, my mother married my stepfather, a man who was full of hostility, anger, and bitterness. My life changed dramatically as a result.

I remember that when my mother dated my stepfather, I didn't approve, and I didn't know what to do about it. I do not remember, however, my mother telling me in advance that she was going to get married. Sud-

*N*ever once did I hear him say that he cared for me or loved me. I don't recall his ever giving me anything. ◆

denly, she and John were married, and John came to live with us. I felt as if he had invaded my life.

After about two weeks, John and I had a disagreement —something about the fried chicken we were having for supper, as I recall it—and he blew up in anger. I realized that living with him was going to be terrible, and my opinion never changed.

In all ways, John was mean and abusive. I never heard him say a positive word about anything. Never once did I hear him say that he cared for me or loved me. I don't recall his

He was so abusive that many nights as a teenager I went to bed with my .22 rifle loaded beside me and the door locked.

ever giving me anything. He was completely full of himself, and the self he was full of was marked by a violent temper and foul language. Spiritually speaking, he said he believed in God, but he rarely went to church.

He was so abusive that many nights as a teenager I went to bed with my .22 rifle loaded beside me and the door locked. I recall a time seeing him on the bed on top of my mother with his hands around her throat as if he was going to strangle her. If I had been able to put my hand on a knife in that moment, I probably would have killed him.

Because of my stepfather's explosive behavior, neither my mother nor I felt comfortable walking into our house when he was there. We were never quite sure what he might do or what might unleash his anger.

Psychologists tell us that the three essentials for a healthy emotional life are a sense of belonging, a sense of real worth and value, and a sense of competency. I didn't have any of those essentials in my life from age nine to age eighteen, when I left home for college.

My home was not the only place I knew to be abusive.

One of my childhood memories is of a time I went to see an aunt and her husband. I got into an argument with my aunt, and I remember Uncle Ervin slapping me so hard that he knocked me several feet across the room. He was killed the next year in a bicycle accident, and I remember thinking as a boy, *I wonder if God did that to you for what you did to me?*

Countless adults today can relate to my experiences. It seems in the last decade, the willingness of our society to admit, confront, and talk about abuse has greatly increased.

We pastors and counselors hear a constant stream of pain in statements such as the following examples:

"I was beaten until I was raw, both physically and emotionally."

"The abuse eventually became so severe that I no longer felt the pain. I was numb most of the time."

"When my father would start abusing me, I'd drift off inside myself and try to think of something else. That was the only way I could manage to cope."

"My mother never once said to me that she approved of anything I did. Instead, I heard about everything I couldn't do, would never be, and shouldn't have said or done."

DIFFERENTIATING BETWEEN DISCIPLINE AND ABUSE

It's critically important as we discuss abuse, and God's words of healing and comfort to those who are abused, to differentiate between discipline and abuse.

The definition of abuse varies from one person to the next. The extent of perceived abuse can also vary from one period in life to the next. To one person, for example, adultery may be regarded as abuse in a marriage; to another, abuse may be thought of only as physical violence.

Verbal abuse and emotional abuse are more difficult to define than physical or sexual abuse. To some, regular or intense criticism might be considered verbal abuse and emotional abuse. To another person, such words of criticism may have no impact at all.

The definition of abuse varies from one person to the next. The extent of perceived abuse can also vary from one period in life to the next.

We must recognize fundamental differences between discipline and abuse.

In the first place, discipline is given in direct response to a person's actions. There should always be an identifiable cause for discipline. Abuse, on the other hand, is frequently unrelated to a victim's behavior. A victim's totally innocent actions may trigger a violent response in an abuser. The person who is abusive has an inner predisposition to abuse. In other words, the abuser is just waiting for an excuse to be abusive. The abuser hits, deprives, or assaults because of something that resides deep within—the abuse erupts out of an inner well of anger, bitterness, or hatred.

In the second place, discipline is administered for the ultimate benefit of the person being disciplined. A spanking or a time-out, for example, might be given to a child to get that child's attention focused on something the child did, in hopes of training the child to change. The goal of discipline is altered behavior and a change in the way a person responds to life. Abuse, on the other hand, seeks to do a victim harm. The abuser's intent is to hurt and to inflict pain. It is not corrective.

At the core of abusive behavior is a desire to control someone else. Abuse is manipulative and based on power.

Discipline is an act of love—rooted in a desire for a person to be the best that person can be.

My mother often used a switch on me, and sometimes I felt she thrashed me because she was angry to a degree that was beyond what my actions had warranted. At times, my legs would bleed. She also kept a very tight rein on me. She wanted to know where I was and what I was doing at every moment of every day.

Still, I have never thought of my mother as being physically abusive. My mother wanted me to grow up to be someone special. While she was pregnant, she regularly went down behind our barn and sat on a stump and prayed for me that God would make me great someday. She prayed for me every day of her life after I was born. My physical punishments were intended for my good. They came as a result of my misbehavior and were intended to change my bad behavior into good behavior.

My stepfather, by contrast, spewed out his hostilities regardless of what was happening around him. He had no concept of my becoming someone better than I was—I doubt if he had that concept for himself.

We can know these things for certain about abuse:

◆ It is never God's desire that His children be ritualistically or regularly injured emotionally or physically. Intense verbal criticism, beatings, and instances of severe deprivation of basic needs (food, water, shelter) can be counted as emotional and/or physical abuse.

◆ It is never God's desire that His children be abused sexually. Incest, adultery, and fornication are all explicitly forbidden in the Scriptures.

What, then, are we as God's children to do if we encounter abuse or if we have experienced abuse in the past?

RESPONSES TO ABUSE

The Lord calls for us to respond to our abuse in several ways—all of which put us into a position for Him to heal us of the damage that has been done to us emotionally, and all of which free us so that we are capable of setting down the emotional baggage that results from abuse.

Response #1: Seek God's guidance

If you are being abused today in a relationship, the first thing you must do is to ask the Lord specifically, "Lord, what would You have me to do? What action do You want me to take?"

There's no pat answer for what to do in an abusive situation. The Lord's direction to you will be highly personalized.

◆ God may tell you to move out of the situation physically. If the Lord directs you to move away from your abuser, keep in mind that physical separation does not necessarily mean that you are disavowing a relationship with the person, that you are divorcing, or that you are seeking to escape all contact with the person.

◆ God may tell you to get counseling from a wise, objective, Bible-honoring counselor. Friends often mirror back to you your own desires. In other cases, they give you their biased, subjective opinion. Seek out someone who can be objective about you and your situation, and who will base advice to you on God's Word.

◆ God may tell you to stay in the situation, pray, and

believe in a transformation of life for the other person and for your relationship. Nothing in the Scriptures requires you to continue to stay in the presence of those who abuse you or to continue to associate with those who have abused you in the past. The Lord may ask you, however, to stand firm in your relationship with Him, stay in the relationship, and continue to speak the Word of the Lord to the person abusing you.

I believe when you pray and ask God for specific guidance, He will give it to you. He will cause your mind and heart to gravitate toward a solution or a course of action that will seem right to you. You'll have a clear understanding of what you are to do or say, and you'll also experience a deep inner peace.

Response #2: Pray for your abuser

Whether your experience with abuse is in the past or present, you must begin to pray for your abuser.

As you pray for an abuser, ask the Lord to give you insights into the cause of the abusive behavior. Even as you pray, recognize that the person who is being abused is rarely the cause. Oh, the abuser may say that the victim is responsible, but in fact, the abuser must be held accountable for the actions and must be responsible for what is inflicted.

The Lord may give you a deep compassion that will cause you to want to enter into intercessory prayer for the person. He may reveal to you incidents in the abuser's past that need to be brought to the surface where the abuser can face them squarely and seek godly counsel.

In the case of my stepfather, I came to know later in life that his father had kept him down on the farm to work instead of letting him go to college, which he had very much wanted to do. Thus, he had been kept from becoming the medical doctor he longed to be. My stepfather no doubt felt great anger toward his father for denying him the career he wanted. He allowed his anger to be channeled in inappropriate ways. Even when he might have pursued medicine at a later time, he allowed his anger to consume him to the point that he had to settle for menial odd jobs instead.

Knowing that about my stepfather did not cause my stepfather to change. It didn't lessen my abhorrence for the abuse he inflicted upon my mother and me. But it did give me an insight into my stepfather that allowed me to feel greater compassion for him.

The Lord may also give you insights into what you might do to help the person. He may reveal to you something that is currently happening in the abuser's life:

◆ Is the abuser under extreme pressure or stress?

◆ Has the abuser experienced a recent tragedy or life-shaking event?

◆ Has the abuser developed a habit of criticism, such that the person really isn't aware of how cutting the words may be?

Asking these questions is a matter not of excusing the behavior of an abuser but of seeking God's wisdom in how best to pray for the person and respond to the person. Ask the Lord, "How can I respond to this person in a way that is loving and righteous before You?"

At the root of all abuse are several factors. I'll mention two.

First, the abusive person has an intense restlessness, an agitation, or a festering wound. Something is deeply wrong inside the person who is abusive. Hurt, doubt, worry, hatred, bitterness, or anger is unresolved and likely has been unresolved for a long period of time.

Only God can calm that restlessness with His peace.

Only God can heal that hatred with His love.

Only God can deal with that doubt or worry with His presence.

Only God can resolve that anger or bitterness with His forgiveness.

Pray that the person will come into a relationship with the Lord Jesus. If the person professes to have such a relationship, pray that the Lord will deal with the heart in the specific area of hurt or injury, and that the Lord will convict the person of the error in inflicting abuse on others.

Second, the abusive person rarely expects to be confronted. Power and control are the core issues to the abusive person. Abusers expect their victims to run away and hide, whimper, cave in, cry, shrink back, or fall silent. One of the most beneficial things you can do for yourself as a victim and for the abuser is to stand up to the abuser and say, "That's enough."

If it means leaving the house, leave.

If it means refusing to listen to the harangue of criticism, walk out of the room.

If it means standing up to the person, stand up to the person.

For example, if a person criticizes you intensely, say, "Listen, what is it about me that is really at the core of what you dislike? Do you realize that you are constantly at me about something? Is it because something is eating away at you? Is there something you don't like about yourself that is behind the way you criticize me?"

Ask for specifics. Ask for specific reasons for the abusive behavior and for specific changes that must be made if you are to continue in the relationship. Insist that the person deal with you and the situation at hand in a calm, rational, direct manner. Don't talk to the person until the person can talk with you calmly and rationally. Require the person to hear that you are feeling abused and that you will not allow yourself to be abused any further. If the abuser is incapable of a rational discussion with you, or if you lack the courage, strength, or communication skills to insist upon such an encounter, ask another person or a group of people to join with you in forcing an encounter.

Doing nothing is not wise. Simply taking the abuse repeatedly is unproductive and unhealthy—for you and the abuser.

Intervening in a person's abusive behavior is actually an act of love for that person. It is saying to the person, "I don't want to see you so violently unhappy. I want to see you live in a way that is not marked by repetitive abusive behavior—either verbal or physical. I want to see you become whole in Christ Jesus."

The most awesome thing you can ever do is to turn your abuser over to God and to say to Him, "I am committing this person to You. I trust You to deal with this person." God knows exactly how to deal with your enemies.

The most sobering thing you can ever say to an abuser is, "I will no longer take your abuse. I'm trusting God to defend me. I'm turning you over to Him, and I'm trusting that He will deal with you."

Response #3: Don't blame God for the abuse

Some victims seem to believe that God might be using the abusive behavior of another person to teach them something or to remove some type of sin from their lives. That is not God's way! God never uses an evil means for a righteous end. Abuse is contrary to God's desire. It has nothing to do with God's will. He never promotes abusive behavior or approves of it.

The devil would like nothing better than for you to blame God for your abuse. Soon, he'll have you believing that God has caused everything bad you've ever experienced. And shortly after that, he'll have you convinced that God is out to get you rather than to love you, redeem you, and shower you with His blessings.

Jesus said clearly, "The thief [the devil] does not come except to steal, and to kill, and to destroy. I have come that they may have life, and that they may have it more abundantly" (John 10:10).

If you're going to blame anybody for allowing your abuse, blame the devil, who not only plants the seeds of hatred and bitterness in a person's heart but waters and cultivates them regularly!

The most sobering thing you can ever say to an abuser is, "I will no longer take your abuse."

Response #4: Forgive your abuser

Perhaps the most important thing that you can do, and must do, is to forgive your abuser.

Forgiveness is the way to bring peace into your heart. No matter what another person has done to you, you can be free of the impact of the abuse through forgiveness. If you don't forgive, you will be drained continually by memories of that abuse. Those memories will sap your emotional strength and eventually leave you feeling devastated and without emotional resources.

Forgiveness is a must if you are to be healthy.

Furthermore, forgiveness is something that the Lord commands us to do. And He commands us to do it for our sake. He says, "Forgive, and you will be forgiven." When we let others go, we are also freed in our spirits to go on with the lives that God has prepared for us to live.

You do not need to feel like forgiving in order to forgive. In no place in the Bible will you find that feelings and forgiveness are linked. Forgiveness is a choice that you make with your will.

Jesus says, "Believe Me." We choose to believe with our wills. We choose to forgive with our wills.

We don't have to feel something is true in order for it to be true or for us to have a conviction in our wills that it is true. By the same principle, our feelings can very often get us into trouble. We feel uneasy, so we begin to doubt. We feel troubled, so we begin to worry. We feel bad, so we conclude that we aren't forgiven or that we haven't pleased God.

Guilt is a feeling.

Doubt is a feeling.

Worry is a feeling.

Although God is concerned about those things, He also tells us that we are not to let feelings rule our lives. We are to respond to our feelings with our wills and bring our feelings into line with what God's Word says about us and about our relationship with God.

Even if you don't feel like forgiving someone who has abused you, you can say to the Lord today, "Lord, I choose to forgive today. I choose to release this person from my heart and put the person in Your hands."

Ask yourself, "Have I truly forgiven my abuser and turned the person over to God?" If so, you have fulfilled what is required of you. You do not need to become close to the person or pretend that nothing has happened between the two of you. You do not need to put yourself back into a position where the person can abuse you again.

Response #5: Forgive the person who may have allowed your abuse

Very often people who were abused by one parent hold deep resentment against the other parent because they perceive that the parent allowed their abuse. Choose to forgive the parent you believe may have stood by and watched.

Ask the Lord to give you compassion for that other parent or that bystander. That person also may have been a victim. That person may have been emotionally, psychologically, or spiritually incapable of taking action.

Ask the Lord to give you insight into the bystander's

Choose to forgive the parent you believe may have stood by and watched.

motives. Talk to the bystander about what happened. In talking about your hurt, you will no doubt gain valuable insights that can help you pray more effectively and forgive more freely.

I asked my mother just a few years ago why she married my stepfather. She replied, "I felt you needed a father." My mother made a mistake, but her motives were not in error. She had not planned for me to be abused. She did not give assent to my stepfather's abusive behaviors. She no doubt defended me more than I will ever know.

Again, knowing my mother's motives didn't change the fact of the abuse we both received, but it did help me see that my mother had been victimized twice—she was abused, and the very person she attempted to help was abused!

Response #6: Choose the truth about yourself and about your abuser

One of the greatest lies that abused people frequently swallow whole is the lie that they deserved the abuse they received. Nobody deserves to be manipulated or injured, or to have self-esteem, identity, and sense of value smashed into a billion bits.

Parents who continally tell their children that they are worth nothing and never will amount to anything are abusive parents. If you have told your child that, recognize what you have done to your child, and seek to make amends with your child—no matter how old he or she may be.

If you were told that repeatedly as a child, recognize that your parents did not tell you God's truth. God's truth is that you are worth something—you are even worth the death of His only beloved Son, Jesus Christ. You are His child now. You are a joint heir with Christ Jesus—in other words, God considers you to be so valuable that He is willing for you to share in Jesus' full inheritance and to have at your access all of the riches of His eternal kingdom.

In cases of repetitive parental criticism, the comments become a message that a person continues to play and replay over and over and over again in the mind. Those messages are like a cassette tape that gets stuck in a tape deck. When abused people find themselves in an abusive situation, they frequently begin to play the victim tape. They hear all of the old messages. For example: "You can't do it," "You aren't worthy of it," "You'll never be able to handle it," "You aren't good enough," and "You deserve what you're getting."

We must take action to change the messages on the victim tape! First, we must say to ourselves, "That's a lie!" We need to recognize the lies that we have been told and face them squarely. Each time we realize we're thinking, *I'm just not good enough*, we need to say, "Stop the tape! That's a lie."

And after we have called the lie for what it is, we must put a new message on the tape: "The truth of the matter is, I can do all things through Christ Jesus. The truth of the matter is, I am a joint heir in Christ Jesus of all God's benefits. The truth of the matter is, I am in line to receive God's rewards. The truth of the matter is, Christ in me has the power, strength, and ability. Together, we will succeed in this."

In my life, I had a tape that told me all the things that I couldn't do and could never become. I recognized that the tape was playing in my head one day, and I said right out loud, "That's no longer true. That may have been partially true about Charles Stanley in the past, but that's no longer the truth of my life. Here's the truth . . . ," and I proceeded to put a new message on the tape.

Response #7: Open yourself to God's healing of your abused emotions

Ask God to continue to heal you so that even the memory of an abusive situation or relationship does not bring torment.

Many people who are abused continue to suffer from nightmares or a sudden onslaught of overwhelming memories years, even decades, after the abuse first occurred. If you are experiencing this, it is vitally important that you develop a habit of filling your mind with God's Word, especially just before you go to bed at night.

Listen to messages—either spoken or musical ones—that fill your mind with God's Word and statements of God's love, goodness, grace, and kindness toward you. You may want to listen to tapes of the Bible or tapes of praise music. You may want to read God's Word aloud to yourself. Go to bed with your mind focused on God's Word and His love for you.

If memories of abuse haunt you, address them in the name of Jesus. Ask the Lord to drive those memories from your mind. Say to Him, "Lord, I'm trusting You to turn my thoughts toward what is good, right, and beneficial for me." And then find something to read or to think about that is truly of the Lord.

The Bible tells us that we have been given spiritual authority for "casting down arguments and every high thing that exalts itself against the knowledge of God, bringing every thought into captivity to the obedience of Christ" (2 Cor. 10:5).

The Bible also tells us: "Whatever things are true, whatever things are noble, whatever things are just, whatever things are pure, whatever things are lovely, whatever things are of good report, if there is any virtue and if there is anything praiseworthy—meditate on these things" (Phil. 4:8).

As soon as you recall a painful memory of abuse or rejection, keep these two verses in mind. First, you have the authority to take captive those hurtful memories and to say to them, "You are not of God, and you no longer have a place in my mind. I give you to Christ Jesus, and I choose to think of what He has done for me rather than what has been done to me by others."

Second, you have the ability to think about something else. Literally shut your mind off to the memory of the past, and force yourself to think about something that is true, noble, just, pure, or lovely. Think about good reports—the good news that you have heard or the good experiences of your life. Think about things that are praiseworthy and that are pleasing to God.

Response #8: Refuse to retaliate

I was sitting at the dinner table one night eating supper with my mother and stepfather. I said something—I don't remember what—and my stepfather slapped me across the face.

I was fifteen years of age. For six years, I had seen the man abuse my mother physically, but before that night he had never slapped me. His abuse of me had been verbal and emotional. There were times when he had been on the verge of hitting me, but Mom had always intervened, no doubt taking the abuse later in my place.

When he slapped me that night, something inside me snapped. I slapped him back as hard as I could.

It was disastrous. Why? Because my stepfather didn't hit me back. From that moment I knew that I was in control. And no fifteen-year-old boy has any business being in control of any family. My feeling of being in control turned into a rebellious spirit.

I was a Christian at that time. I had accepted the Lord Jesus as my Savior, and I was reading the Bible and seeking to obey God. Still, I developed a rebellious spirit. Just because someone is no longer rebelling against God doesn't mean that the person is immune to rebelling against other human beings. A Christian can rebel against another person just as readily as an unsaved person can.

And rebellion, if it isn't dealt with, can become very heavy emotional baggage.

God's Word gives us no privilege or right to take vengeance into our hands. In fact, God's Word tells us that the privilege of vengeance belongs solely to God. Deuteronomy 32:35 clearly states of God, "Vengeance is Mine, and recompense."

Don't allow the sin of an abuser against you to become

a root of sin in your life. Refuse to vent your hurt and anger on your abuser. Remember the command of the Lord in Romans 12:21: "Do not be overcome by evil, but overcome evil with good."

The best thing we can do—for ourselves, from God's perspective, and for the transformation of the abuser—is to follow these words from the Bible:

> If your enemy is hungry, give him bread to eat;
> And if he is thirsty, give him water to drink;
> For so you will heap coals of fire on his head,
> And the LORD will reward you (Prov. 25:21–22).

An act of kindness toward your abuser brings you a reward, and it frees God to deal with your abuser directly.

Response #9: Choose to go forward in your life positively

In leaving for college at the age of eighteen, I feared for the safety of my mother. Nevertheless, I knew I needed to go.

Never let an abuser dictate the course of your life or keep you from doing what you know the Lord is leading you to do. Part of moving forward in your life is believing that the cycle of abuse in your family has been broken—and is being broken—by your change of behavior.

Psychologists and behavioral researchers have discovered a very high correlation between those who abuse and those who were abused. As Christians, we can choose, however, to pattern ourselves after our heavenly Father—who is never abusive—rather than after an abusive earthly parent or some other abusive person. We can say, as a prayer and as an expression of the will, "I choose to be a loving, giving person. I ask You, Father, to free me from the chains of abuse I have experienced in the past and to transform me into Your likeness emotionally and psychologically. Break the cycle of abuse in my family history, and begin with me. Don't allow me to become an abusive parent. Don't allow me to treat others around me as victims of my hostility, anger, or bitterness. Turn me into a person who is more and more like Your Son, Jesus Christ."

The cycle of abuse must come to an end in Christ Jesus. No Christian has the option to say, "That's just the way I am. I was abused as a child, and that's why I do what I do today."

The true Christ-centered response is to say, "That may be the way I was, but I am redeemed by Christ Jesus. I am in the process of being transformed into His image. I am in the process of being healed."

The true Christ-centered response is to say, "That may be the way I was, but I am redeemed by Christ Jesus."

✳

Response #10: Look for God to bring something good out of your experience

Trust God to work something good out of that abusive situation or experience you have endured. If you are physically assaulted or beaten down verbally, you can and must turn immediately to God and say, "Lord, You see how I have been wounded. I trust You to be my defender and to exact Your revenge in this situation. I trust You to heal me and to restore me. I trust You to bring justice out of this situation. I trust You to cause something good to happen in my life as the result of this—that I will grow and not wither, I will become stronger and not weaker, I will become more like You and not shrink in my faith."

Also look for added meaning—for truths that are in keeping with God's Word.

My mother once told me that on the day she married John, she promised God that she'd never leave him, and she didn't. Even at the end of his life, when he was blind and truly in need of nursing care, she stood by him and took care of him until he died. I never heard her say anything bad about John, despite the abuse we both received.

My mother's response to John was a great example to me of steadfastness, faithfulness, and determination. My mother was like a tank. She was always moving forward slowly and steadily.

In many ways, my mother's response to John is like the response of the Lord to those who continually reject Him and abuse His name, thwart His purposes on the earth, or speak ill of Him. The Lord continues to move toward those people with love. He does not allow their nature to change His nature. And in that is perhaps the greatest lesson the abused person can learn about the self. The lesson is this: You are a lovable person.

If you are a victim of abuse today, let me be the first to assure you: You are loved by God. You are loved by your fellow Christians. You are worthy to be loved.

Not because of what you have done.

Not because of what has been done to you.

But because of who you are—a child of God, fully

adopted into His family, and fully deserving of the love of your fellow brothers and sisters in Christ Jesus.

Speak God's love to yourself today. Say aloud, "I am God's child. He loves me—yes, me!" Let the truth of those words sink deep into your soul. Let them heal the hurt you have known and the shame you may have felt. Let God's love for you wipe away your tears and restore you to wholeness.

TRUTH CAPSULE

When memories of abuse overwhelm you, or you find yourself the victim of abuse . . .

1. Run to Jesus. His arms are open wide to you, and He will always receive you with love.
2. Do what the Lord tells you to do with regard to your abuser. Ask Him to guide you. Ask Him to help you pray for your abuser with wisdom and compassion. Ask Him to help you forgive your abuser as well as the one who stood by and did nothing while you were being abused.
3. Open yourself up to the Lord's healing power. Choose to be healed. Ask the Lord to give you the strength to trust the situation to Him and to let go of your desires for vengeance and retaliation.
4. Trust the Lord to bring you to a greater experience of wholeness and spiritual strength than you have ever known.

*M*y excess baggage from abuse.

_____

_____

_____

_____

_____

_____

_____

_____

_____

*H*ow I can lighten this load.

_____

_____

_____

_____

_____

_____

_____

_____

_____

*G*od is the source of my strength.

Words
of
comfort
and
healing
to
those
who
are
feeling

INFERIOR

When I was in sixth grade, I attended a school where either you had to pass all of the subjects you took, or you had to repeat the grade. In what must have been an attempt to motivate us toward passing, my sixth-grade teacher drew several pictures on the chalkboard—an airplane, a train, a ship, an automobile, and then a field of sheep.

If you made *A*'s, the teacher wrote your name in large letters under the picture of the airplane. And so it went, right down the line through *B, C,* and *D* grades. If you made an *F* in any one of the six or seven subjects taught that year, she put your name in large letters in the sheep field.

Many days I would walk into the classroom and look on the board to find that the only name in the sheep field was Charles Stanley.

My teacher's actions reinforced what I was hearing at home from my stepfather, who repeatedly told me that I wasn't good for anything, wasn't worth anything, and would

My teacher's actions reinforced what I was hearing at home from my stepfather, who repeatedly told me that I wasn't good for anything, wasn't worth anything, and would never amount to anything. ◆

never amount to anything. I tried very hard to please my stepfather, but no matter what I did, it was never quite good enough for his notice, much less his approval. Furthermore, in his opinion, I couldn't do anything at all!

I internalized a message that became emotional baggage in my life: "You're not worth much, and you don't belong with the rest of the members of your class. You're not as good as those around you."

Several other factors compounded that message and turned it into a genuine, full-blown inferiority complex.

One of those factors was that I had started school a year before my peers, so I was always the youngest person in my class, and therefore, I also tended to be the smallest child and the skinniest. Many times that led to my being picked on or left out.

Another factor was that my mother made me wear short pants until I went to junior high school, and then I wore knickers and long socks. Nobody else wore knickers!

Yet another factor was that among the many places we lived while I was growing up, several of our homes were basement apartments. From my child's perspective, anybody who lived higher than we did seemed to be more important. I grew up feeling intimidated by anyone that I felt was of greater status in the community.

Those factors alone, of course, would not have been sufficient to make me feel inferior if I had been receiving an equal amount of praise and encouragement from other sources. Unfortunately, any sources of positive self-esteem-building input were rare and far between.

I remember only two people in my life, other than my

mom, who registered any signs of approval of me during my growing-up years.

One was a schoolteacher named Mrs. Ferrell. She was a tall dark-haired woman. One afternoon as I was walking out of her room, I overheard her say to another teacher, "I like Charles." That was all I remember her saying. No doubt they had been discussing me and my shortcomings, but I happened to come along just as the teacher made one positive comment about me. It still rings in my ears. Those three simple words, "I like Charles," meant something to me.

The other person who showed me that he approved of me was a Sunday school teacher I had during my childhood years when I attended the Pentecostal Holiness church. His name was Craig Stowe. Even after I had joined the Baptist church as a teenager and he was no longer my Sunday school teacher, Craig Stowe would stop me on the street and buy a newspaper from me.

I still remember his pulling up in his automobile and saying to me as he paid for his newspaper, "Charles, I just want you to know I've been thinking about you, and I pray for you often." It didn't take me long to figure out that Craig Stowe didn't need to buy a newspaper from me. He had the newspaper delivered to his home. Still, he cared about me enough to stop on his way home and to give me a word of encouragement. Furthermore, he always gave me more than the newspaper cost and told me to keep the change. He was the only man during all my growing-up years who conveyed to me, "I love you and I care for you and I'm thinking about you."

Those two voices stand out like beacons in a wilderness

of disapproval and devaluing statements that I heard frequently and that always found their way to the core of my being. They created low self-esteem and feelings of inadequacy—a major form of bondage and very heavy emotional baggage, indeed.

Many people carry that baggage today. They express it in myriad ways. For example:

"Nobody ever cared."

"Any success I have today is because of what I have done, not because of anything my parents or teachers did."

"My dad always told me to lift myself up by my bootstraps like he did. I don't think he realized that he was responsible for giving me the basic bootstraps of life!"

"I don't know why it was so hard for my mother to give a little word of praise. Anytime she said, 'That was good,' it was as if she was choking on her words. She may have been saying, 'Good job,' but her actions and the way she said those words told me she was lying to me."

No child asks to grow up without a sense of self-value. No child is born with low self-esteem. Children who have an inferiority complex get it from somewhere and from somebody. Usually, it's from the home.

If you are a parent reading this, recognize that you and your spouse are number one in your children's eyes. Your opinion counts more than anybody else's. What you say about your children to them has a great impact on how they will see themselves all the way into adulthood and sometimes for their entire lives.

Parents do a great disservice to their children in allowing them to base their likes and dislikes on peer opinion or na-

No child is born with low self-esteem. Children who have an inferiority complex get it from somewhere and from somebody.

tional advertising campaigns without some type of parental intervention. The damage is threefold:

1. Children go into debt for things they do not need but want because they are told they should want them.
2. Children base their behavior on other people's opinions rather than on God's opinion.
3. Children begin to rely on things to satisfy them rather than on a relationship with God, which is the only thing that can truly satisfy their deep inner longings.

Recognize that it is your responsibility as a parent to tell your children how to interpret messages from others, including media messages. Interject your opinion, your ideas, and your words of encouragement. Build up your children so that they can withstand peer and cultural pressures to conform to standards that are unlike God's Word. Your words go a long way in assisting your children to differentiate between the hype of this world and the help of God's Word.

WHOSE OPINION REALLY COUNTS?

Many people come from backgrounds in which they were taught—subtly or very directly—that they would never amount to anything, weren't worth anything, and would never be fully acceptable. Look around you on any given day, and you'll find people who don't think they can dress well enough, talk well enough, think fast enough, look good enough, or do things well enough to be truly of value.

This feeling of inadequacy is just that—a feeling. And the Bible tells us that we are to base our opinions not on feelings but on the fact of God's Word. When we allow ourselves to feel inadequate, we are denying what God Himself says about us.

On the other hand, when we get our focus off what we think—or what others think about us—and get our eyes on who God says we are and what God thinks about us, self-esteem automatically begins to rise.

God bases our worth not on what we have but on who we have, Jesus Christ as our personal Savior and the Holy Spirit as our ever-present Comforter and Counselor.

God bases our worth not on our performance or achievements but on whether we have received His free gift of grace and forgiveness in our lives.

God bases our worth not on who we know or where we live or how we look but on whether we know, follow, and trust Jesus Christ as our Lord.

Our society continually bombards us with messages that we need to wear a certain type of jeans, drive a certain type of car, and use a certain brand of toothpaste and mouthwash for us to be acceptable members of society.

God says we need only to receive His love and to accept what He has done for us in order for us to be fully acceptable in His eternal kingdom.

Now, whose messages are you receiving into your life? On whose opinion are you basing your self-appraisal of value? On the world's opinion, which is shallow, nearly always wrong, and destructive and detrimental far more often than it is helpful? Or are you basing your self-worth on God's opinion, which is eternal and always for your benefit?

Have you based your life on the opinion or words of your earthly father and mother? Or are you basing your identity on the opinion and Word of your heavenly Father?

Let me share with you a significant verse of the Bible. The apostle Paul wrote to the believers in Ephesus: "We are His workmanship, created in Christ Jesus for good works, which God prepared beforehand that we should walk in them" (Eph. 2:10). Perhaps no verse in the Bible so succinctly and clearly tells you that God sees you as a precious person, someone who is extremely important to Him.

Note several things about that verse. First, you are God's workmanship. The word in the original Greek in which the verse was written literally means "a person of notable excellence." You may say, "Well, I don't look excellent," or "I don't do excellent things," or "I'm not excellent at anything." That's not what God says! He calls you a person of notable excellence because *He made you.* You need to see yourselves as God sees you—a prized example of His creation.

Second, God's creation of you is *in Christ Jesus.* God loved you so much that He gave His only begotten Son, Jesus Christ, to die on a cross for you so that when you believe on Him, you might have eternal life.

God's love for you can never grow any greater. It can never be diminished. It can never be extended. It is always the same—*infinite!*

Your creation in Christ Jesus is actually a re-creation of you. As Paul wrote elsewhere, "If anyone is in Christ, he is a new creation; old things have passed away; behold, all things have become new" (2 Cor. 5:17).

A part of being a new creation in Christ Jesus means getting rid of the old creation—especially the messages about past sins and inabilities, incapacities, and inferiority.

It was not until I was an adult that I realized I was looking up to certain people for the wrong reasons. I was not admiring them for who they were in the Lord. Rather, I was feeling intimidated by them for who they were in the commu-nity—compared to who I felt I was. Once again, I recognized that I had allowed a lousy tape to play in my mind—a mes-sage that I seemed to push into the cassette player of my psyche every time I met someone who had achieved any de-gree of success.

When I realized what I was doing, I chose to erase that tape! In its place, I put a new message: "I am a new creation, a child of God. I am somebody in Christ. I live on the top floor of God's mansions, and I enjoy the company of angels and saints!"

In recognizing that you are a new creation in Christ Jesus, you must also face up to the fact that Christ does the re-creating. You don't do it. It is His work.

True contentment with yourself means that you no longer strive to be something that you weren't created to be— for example, to look a way you don't look or do something you aren't inclined to do for the sake of acceptance by others. True contentment rises above self-improvement programs. Ultimately, God has the best self-improvement plan. It's to-tally in keeping with your identity. His is the only plan that re-creates you in a positive, eternally lasting, completely bene-ficial, no-damaging-side-effects way!

If you are suffering from feelings of inferiority today, say to the Lord, "Lord, whatever potential I have, I trust You to bring it to fullness. You alone know all that I'm capable of doing. You alone know how to release my potential and turn it into reality. You alone know what circumstances, challenges, opportunities, and encounters will be required for my poten-tial to be fulfilled. I am trusting You to bring about those things in my life. I'll do whatever You show me to do. I'll work hard at whatever job You give me. But as of today, I cease to try to be perfect on my own. I give up my striving for perfection in my own strength."

Third, the Lord has created you for *good works*, and He is the One who enables you to do them. The Lord has already designed what those good works are to be. In other words, God had a purpose in mind for you even before you were born. He had a role for you to fill, a niche for you to occupy, a place for you to live as His person on this earth.

If you ever catch a glimpse of how much God loves you, desires to be with you, and has prepared good things for you, you'll find yourself with confidence and inner assurance that can't be matched. It won't matter to you if another person turns you down or turns away from you because you know without a shadow of a doubt that God loves you! It's wonder-ful, of course, if the other person likes you and responds to you, but if the person doesn't, you can still have the assurance of God's divine and unchanging love.

Many people who feel inferior have a very difficult time accepting expressions of approval from other people. When

God had a purpose in mind for you even before you were born. He had a role for you to fill.

they hear words of praise, they start thinking about all the ways in which they don't deserve the attention or friendship of the person giving the praise—they dwell on the ways in which they haven't measured up, aren't qualified, can't live up to certain expectations, or don't meet certain standards. God's approval of them is based not on what they do or achieve but on their relationship with Him. Once people begin to accept God's approval of them, they frequently find that they can accept more readily the compliments and praise of others.

Above all, you need to remind yourself constantly who God says you are and what He thinks of you. Your self-esteem must be based on His opinion, not someone else's opinion or even your opinion. Your self-esteem is to be based on what God thinks. And God thinks you are fantastic!

GETTING A GODLY PERSPECTIVE ON PERFECTION

A person who suffers from an inferiority complex tends to respond to life in several ways:

◆ He may continually ridicule others, attempting to bring them down to his level.

◆ She may constantly downgrade herself in the presence of others or engage in self-deprecating behaviors—even to the point of ceasing to care about her appearance, engaging in immoral activities, or failing to fulfill the most basic responsibilities.

◆ He may ardently seek peer approval to the point that he is willing to engage in illegal or immoral activities.

◆ She may strive for perfection in an attempt to compensate for earlier perceived failures.

The first three responses are fairly obvious and can usually be remedied by the person's recognition of the actions.

The last response—striving for perfection—is much more difficult for someone with an inferiority complex to recognize. Such a person is less likely to appraise abilities and attributes realistically. Feeling worth nothing and incapable of anything but failure, the perfectionist seeks to succeed at all costs. Such a person's expectations and understanding of perfection are usually ill-defined.

The truth is that nobody can live up to God's perfection.

Nobody can do what is right all the time.

Nobody can live a totally sin-free life.

Nobody can escape all temptation.

God's Word clearly spells out the human condition when it says, "All have sinned and fall short of the glory of God" (Rom. 3:23).

We live in physical bodies that are operated by the physical senses. As fleshly people living in a fallen world, we are always going to have temptations and struggles.

That fact is so discouraging to some people that they opt never to try to line up their lives with God's Word. They yield to their circumstances, the culture, or the devil's temptation to sin. They disobey God. They experience no peace, no fulfillment, no sense of God's presence and power in their lives. And in the final analysis, they live their entire lives feeling inadequate.

The good news is that we do not need to live with a

spirit of inadequacy. God says that in Christ Jesus, we are adequate! We are covered with His identity, and in accepting Jesus as our personal Savior and Lord, we take on His image so that when the Father looks at us, He no longer sees our weaknesses, our faults, and our frailties. Instead, He sees the person of Jesus. He sees His strengths, His perfection, and His uncompromising goodness.

On the cross, Jesus Christ made all the provision necessary totally to take care of your guilt and your sin. They are removed from your life when you accept His sacrifice on the cross as being a sacrifice made for you.

What is the alternative to being with Christ? It is despair and utter discouragement at all turns.

GOD DOESN'T EXPECT YOU TO GET IT RIGHT ALL THE TIME

In accepting Jesus Christ, and in trading in our inadequacy for His adequacy, we are—as the Scriptures tell us—born again. We have the opportunity to start over with a clean slate. And just as a newborn baby has to learn certain skills in life, so we are to learn how to do certain things in the spiritual realm.

The very idea that God calls us children indicates to me that He knows that we have a lot to learn—and that in the process of learning, we are going to fall occasionally and scrape ourselves and skin our knees. He knows that we are not going to be perfect Christians and that we are going to falter, fail, and fall. His grace is sufficient for that!

In I John 2:1, we read, "My little children, these things I write to you, so that you may not sin." But then the verse goes on to say, "And if anyone sins, we have an Advocate with the Father, Jesus Christ the righteous." It's as if God is saying to us, "Little children, I don't want you to sin. I've given you My Word so that you can grow up and avoid sinning. But if and when you sin, I've made provision for that, too."

We can't be perfect and we won't ever be perfect, but we can enjoy the perfection of Christ Jesus. We can accept His loving-kindness. We can acknowledge that He doesn't expect us to be perfect, but He does expect us to keep growing in Him, to stay in relationship with Him, and to keep trusting Him day by day. He says that as we do that, He will work out His perfection in us. We won't have to struggle to do it, strive to do it, or knock ourselves out to do it. He'll do the work. He'll bring about His perfection in us in His timing, using His methods, and all for His purposes!

Nobody can be the best always. Nobody comes in first every time. Nobody gets it right each time. It's physically and emotionally impossible for a pitcher to pitch all strikes, a pianist to hit all the right notes in every concert, or a police officer to make the right judgment call in each and every arrest.

If you are seeking to be perfect, not only are you seeking to do something that is impossible, but you are saying to yourself and to God, "I'm not satisfied with the way I'm made. I'm made with the capacity and the ability to fail. I have flaws. I have weaknesses. I'm not perfect. And I don't like it."

As long as people hold to that position, they will be miserable. And they also put themselves beyond the reach of God to help them.

The apostle Paul wrote that the Lord had spoken to him one time with these words: "My grace is sufficient for you, for My strength is made perfect in weakness" (2 Cor. 12:9). In other words, Paul's personal human weaknesses were God's opportunity to reveal His strength.

It's in our times of failure that we have the capacity to grow the most. It's when we know what we have done wrong that we see more clearly what is right to do. It's when we have fallen short that we are put into a position to trust God to cover our shortfall. It's when we can't succeed in our ability that we are in a position to rely on the Lord.

This is not to say that we are to fail purposefully or that we are to become lax or lazy. It is to say that we must face our inner compulsions to succeed, to win, and to be perfect. We must recognize that unless we trust God for our success —both to define it for us and to help us achieve it—we will never be truly successful.

GOD DOESN'T EXPECT YOU TO REACH YOUR DEFINITION OF POTENTIAL

One day I saw a young person with a long face, and I asked her, "What's the problem?"

She said, "Well, I didn't do very well on the test I just took."

"Oh?"

"Yes," she said, "I only got a *B*. That's not good enough."

"Why isn't it good enough?"

"Because I should have earned an *A*."

"Why?"

"Because I should always do my best."

"Did you study?" I asked. "Did you prepare yourself the best you knew to prepare?"

"Yes."

"Then wasn't a *B* a reflection of your best effort on this particular exam?"

"Yes, but it isn't enough. I've got to study more so I can earn an *A*."

Now, I'm not at all decrying a person's desire to learn material as best she can and to score the best she can on a test, but the young person was struggling with a deep-seated problem of perfectionism.

A person who thinks that she always must do the best, have the best, achieve the highest, and own the best has confused the notion of reaching her potential with something unhealthy and unattainable. Such a person usually feels responsible for defining her potential according to what is potentially possible, given ideal circumstances and abundant talent. This becomes the standard; this, and only this, is what's acceptable.

Every person has potential. The problem with potential is that nobody can truly define it for himself or for another person. Only God fully knows, and can thoroughly and accurately define, a person's potential. Furthermore, only God can help a person reach full potential. Nobody can achieve it on his own.

Therefore, we need to stop striving to do what we are incapable of doing and start trusting God to do what only He can do!

GOD DOESN'T GRADE ON THE CURVE

God doesn't grade on the curve. He doesn't compare us to others. He also doesn't judge us according to a sliding scale of righteousness.

Many people compare themselves to others and come away saying, "I don't sin like that guy," or "I'm doing at least as good as she is."

God doesn't grade on the curve. He doesn't compare us to others. He also doesn't judge us according to a sliding scale of righteousness.

Christians frequently say to me—and to other pastors and counselors—such things as these:

"I know I'm not praying as much as I should."

"I know I'm not giving enough."

"I know I'm not reading my Bible as much as I ought."

My comment to them is, "How much is enough?" People need to pray, give, and read the Bible as much as they are able and then trust God that what they have done is sufficient in His hands. If God desires for you to pray more, give more, or read more, He'll direct you to pray about specific things, give a specific amount, read a particular passage, or study a particular subject. God doesn't say, "Do more." He says, "Do this. Do that. Do the other." God deals with us in specifics, not generalities.

If God has called you to do a certain thing and you aren't doing it, you should get busy and obey Him.

If your feelings, however, are ones of inadequacy and of guilt for not being perfect or of not achieving something for God, you need to reappraise and to rethink your position.

God doesn't ask you to perform for Him. He doesn't ask you to try harder. God will never speak from the heavens to you and say, "You aren't doing enough for Me."

God's direction to us is always very specific. He will say, "I want you to teach this Sunday school class," or "I want you to remind that person of My promise in the Word," or "I want you to give this amount to that project." God speaks to us about what He wants us to do *in the present tense* of our lives.

When we have an overwhelming sense that we should do this, ought to do that, or must do the other, we experience false guilt. It's not of God. It's something we require of ourselves or something others have taught us that we are required to do.

WHAT MUST YOU DO TO OVERCOME YOUR FEELINGS OF INFERIORITY?

God's Word offers five guidelines for overcoming deep-seated feelings of inferiority.

Guideline #1: Praise God for your gifts, talents, and abilities

Make a list of all the things you can do well, enjoy doing, and have succeeded in doing. If you have a very low level of self-esteem, you may be able to think of only one or two things. Still, force yourself to write them down.

Don't overlook the simple things that you may assume everybody does or every person is capable of doing.

If you have a great smile, write it down.

If you know how to tell a story well, write it down.

If you are a good cook, write it down.

Recognize that all of your gifts, talents, and abilities come from the Lord. The Bible tells us that He is the "author and finisher of our faith" (Heb. 12:2). It also says that "every good gift and every perfect gift is from above, and comes down from the Father of lights, with whom there is no variation or shadow of turning" (James 1:17).

Take a look at the spiritual growth you have made in your life. That growth is the work of the Lord in your life. It is His manifesting His nature in you. Any gifts that are given to you by the Holy Spirit are worthy to be listed!

Don't be embarrassed as your list grows and grows and grows. This is your list. It is a record of the work of the Lord in your life. It is a praise report of God's grace manifest to you.

As you list your gifts, talents, and abilities—and as you praise God for them—you'll find yourself being healed of your inferiority feelings. They will drop from you like unwanted weights. Instead of seeing yourself as a failure, you'll begin to see yourself as God's work in progress—a masterpiece that is of His creation.

Guideline #2: Thank God for His transforming power

Thank God for doing in your life what only He can do.

Thank Him for being your Potter. Read the word of the Lord to the prophet Jeremiah, and take it as a word from the Lord into your life today:

> The word which came to Jeremiah from the LORD, saying: "Arise and go down to the potter's house, and there I will cause you to hear My words." Then I went down to the potter's house, and there he was, making something at the wheel. And the vessel that he made of clay was marred in the hand of the potter; so he made it again into another vessel, as it seemed good to the potter to make. Then the word of the LORD came to me, saying: "O house of Israel, can I not do with you as this potter?" says the LORD. "Look, as the clay is in the potter's hand, so are you in My hand, O house of Israel!" (Jer. 18:1–6).

Thank God today for the transforming power of the Holy Spirit in your life.

Thank God for pruning you, watering you with His Word, and causing you to bear the fruit of the Spirit: "love, joy, peace, longsuffering, kindness, goodness, faithfulness, gentleness, self-control" (Gal. 5:22–23).

Let your feelings of inadequacy drive you to God. You'll find your adequacy in Him.

Thank God today for the transforming power of the Holy Spirit in your life.

Guideline #3: Obey God's leading

Be willing to go where the Lord directs you to go. Be willing to do what He asks you to do.

He will not lead you into failure; rather, He will lead you into success—again, as the Lord defines success.

He will cause you to enter into paths of righteousness and to be victorious over the enemy of your soul.

He will lead you into spiritual battles over the enemy and enable you to win them.

He will cause you to "grow in the grace and knowledge of our Lord and Savior Jesus Christ" (2 Pet. 3:18) and transform you into the mirror image of the Lord, "from glory to glory" (2 Cor. 3:18).

Choose to follow the Lord's leading in your life. He will lead you toward Himself and toward what is His best and highest good for you. Remind yourself of the healing and comforting words of Psalm 23:

> The LORD is my shepherd;
> I shall not want.
> He makes me to lie down in green pastures;
> He leads me beside the still waters.
> He restores my soul;
> He leads me in the paths of righteousness
> For His name's sake.
> Yea, though I walk through the
>   valley of the shadow of death,
> I will fear no evil;
> For You are with me;

Your rod and Your staff, they comfort me.
You prepare a table before me in
    the presence of my enemies;
You anoint my head with oil;
My cup runs over.
Surely goodness and mercy shall follow me
All the days of my life;
And I will dwell in the house of the LORD
Forever.

Guideline #4: Choose to become an intercessor

Regardless of what you think you can or cannot do,
there's one thing you can always do. You can pray, and you
can become a wellspring of praise on this earth for the Lord.
As Jesus entered the city of Jerusalem on the day we've come
to call Palm Sunday, a group of Pharisees demanded that He
rebuke those who were calling Jesus the Messiah, "the King
who comes in the name of the Lord." Jesus replied to the
Pharisees, "I tell you that if these should keep silent, the
stones would immediately cry out" (Luke 19:40).

You may not think that you can do anything or that you
are worth anything, but let me assure you of this: You can
praise God better than a stone can.

You can also become an intercessor in prayer.

In college I felt there were lots of things that I couldn't
do or was incapable of learning, but I always felt that I could
learn to pray—so that is what I set out to do. I prayed often,
"God, teach me how to pray." That's a good prayer for any of

us to pray, no matter how skilled or unskilled we think we are in prayer.

God responds to our desire to pray with an increased understanding of how to pray more effectively. Hear what James says about this:

> The effective, fervent prayer of a righteous man avails much. Elijah was a man with a nature like ours, and he prayed earnestly that it would not rain; and it did not rain on the land for three years and six months. And he prayed again, and the heaven gave rain, and the earth produced its fruit (James 5:16–18).

You may not have thought of yourself as being in the same league as the prophet Elijah, but James reminds us that he started out with a nature just like ours, and that the power in Elijah's life was one wrought by prayer.

Ask the Lord to guide your prayer life, to empower it, and to cause you to be an effectual prayer warrior. If that is your sole identity on this earth—if it is the only thing you truly succeed at doing—you will have accomplished more than you can ever imagine!

Guideline #5: Become an encourager of others

Finally, you can choose to become an encourager of others.

You can praise the good works of others.

You can become an edifier—one who builds up others and encourages them in their faith walk.

In college I became the encourager of my buddies. I had real confidence in what I believed, and even though I went to a so-called Christian school, most of the time I felt as if I needed to defend my faith and champion the cause of Christ. Looking back, I realize that I didn't know as much about what I believed as I thought I did, but at the same time I was very bold in my beliefs. I came on strong. And students were always coming to me to ask me what I thought about various things or to ask me to pray with them.

I often prayed for those who scoffed at me for praying and believing. My prayer was a very specific one: "God, let something happen to them so they'll need me to pray for them and I can then tell them about You."

As you encourage others, pray for them, and give them insights into God's Word, you'll grow in confidence and self-value. You'll discover that you do have something to give away —you have the Word of God and the Spirit of God resident in you and freely flowing through you to others. The prophet Jeremiah wrote about the children of God that even though they were clay pots, they were as valuable as fine gold (see Lam. 4:2). You, too, are a vessel that God desires to use. He is seeking continually to pour Himself through you to others. Open your mouth and your heart, and begin to encourage people the Lord sends your way.

PLEASING IN GOD'S SIGHT

When you understand that you are a child of God and adopted into His family, you know you are pleasing in His sight.

The apostle Paul wrote to the Romans:

> I beseech you therefore, brethren, by the mercies of God, that you present your bodies a living sacrifice, holy, acceptable to God, which is your reasonable service. And do not be conformed to this world, but be transformed by the renewing of your mind, that you may prove what is that good and acceptable and perfect will of God (Rom. 12:1–2).

The Lord doesn't ask us to be perfect. But He does call us to follow His perfect will.

The Lord doesn't ask us to succeed in the eyes of others. He does ask us to seek to live the life that is acceptable to Him—a life not of achievement but of sacrifice, giving, and complete and utter reliance upon the Lord Jesus Christ.

Jesus never said, "Do your best." He said, "Follow Me."

TRUTH CAPSULE

When you are feeling inferior . . .

1. Seek out what the Lord says about who you are. Make His opinion the only opinion that really matters.

2. Praise God for the work that He is doing in your life, for the abilities, talents, and gifts He has given you, and for His using you as His vessel on this earth.

3. Obey the leading of the Lord and follow His footsteps into the success that He has planned for your life.

4. Become an encourager of others. As you encourage others, you will be encouraged and built up in your inner being.

*M*y excess baggage from feeling inferior.

_____

_____

_____

_____

_____

_____

_____

_____

_____

*H*ow I can lighten this load.

_____

_____

_____

_____

_____

_____

_____

_____

*G*od is the source of my strength.

*Words
of
comfort
and
healing
to
those
who
are
struggling
under
the
weight
of*

5

GUILT

W hen I was a young teenager, I came to a sudden and startling realization that God was in charge of my life.

I was standing in the bathtub. Directly above it was a light cord—a brass fixture holding a bare bulb. The cord was a little frayed. I reached up to turn off the light while I was still standing in the water, but before I could touch it, the phone rang. As it rang three or four times, I got out of the tub and ran to answer it. Nobody was on the line.

I developed a wrong view of God—a view that God was distant from me because He, like others in my life, had left me, abandoned me, given up on me. ◆

As I walked back to the bathroom, dripping water all the way, the tub and that hanging cord were framed by the bathroom doorway before me. I stopped in my tracks, and the thought hit me like a jolt of electricity: *That bathtub and lightbulb could have been my electric chair.* The scene before me looked just like the site of an execution.

I said, "God, You just saved my life. Nobody was on that phone but You." Prior to that moment, I don't think I had ever thought about God as a part of my life.

I had thought a lot about God. I remember lying on my bed and wondering what He was like. I'd try to read the Bible, but I didn't understand much of it. God was very obscure, beyond my ability to comprehend Him.

My mother believed in God, and she was saved. But she didn't talk about Him very much around me. When we prayed, we both used King James English. For years, I thought that was the only way a person could be heard in heaven! In language and in daily living, God seemed very distant.

Not only did I think of God as being remote, but I developed a wrong view of God—a view that God was distant from me because He, like others in my life, had left me, abandoned me, given up on me.

Most children develop their God concept based upon the behavior of their parents. My father had died and left me, and when he died, a little bit of my concept about God was established that said, in effect, "God has left you, too."

My mom worked five days a week and was gone from early morning to late afternoon. I spent long hours alone in an empty house. All of this impacted my concept of God. God wasn't very near. He wasn't very dependable. He wasn't very accessible. I couldn't really count on Him being present when I needed Him. In fact, I wasn't sure who He was or if He knew who I was. I came to believe, "God is away somewhere with somebody else."

I never even thought about God as Father. Father—or, in my case, stepfather—was a concept that was too human, too earthly, too familiar. God was God. Remote, and yet watching and listening.

THE GOD OF THE THOU SHALT NOTS

God was remote, and He was a hard, harsh God from my perspective as a lonely, anxious, insecure child. He was authority—and in that regard, He was very much like my stepfather: mean, abusive, out to put me down and drive me out.

My mother's constant admonition, "Don't do anything that you wouldn't want to be caught doing if Jesus were to come," really put a crimp in my style. Just about everything that a normal boy would consider to be fun, my mother and the church considered to be a sin.

Reading the funnies was a sin (and I was delivering the newspapers and longing to see what had happened to Dick Tracy from one day to the next).

Wearing a tie clasp was a sin.

Listening to any kind of music other than hymns was a sin (a bitter pill for a young guy who really enjoyed listening to the popular songs).

Holiness was a terrible burden to strive to live up to—and it resulted in a spirit of striving that infected every area of my life.

I had seen God's hand at work to the point that I had the faith to believe in Him. Still, God was such a mystery that I never truly felt He was accessible to me.

In striving to be holy enough for God to come closer, of

course, I never felt as if I had done enough or was enough to please God. There was always a dark feeling that something bad was about to happen.

No matter how much I read the Bible, I could have read it more.

No matter how much I had prayed, I could have prayed more—even all night.

And even if I prayed all night, I could have done still more. I could have fasted, too!

In my first Bible—a Thompson Chain-Reference® Bible that cost fifteen dollars and was just like gold to me—I wrote these words: "Given to me by my mother who taught me both the love and the wrath of God." I should have circled and underlined the word *wrath*.

Yes, God was a God of judgment. I had no doubt about that as a young boy. God kept points, checked score, took roll. The message about God was one closely connected with images of hell, the importance of the Ten Commandments, and the awesome consequences of sin. It was a concept of God that became emotional baggage and true spiritual bondage for me—for nearly fifty-seven years!

You see, the difficulty with striving to get good enough for God is that the scale keeps sliding. Seeking to be holy is a little like being a high jumper. You clear one height, and the next thing you know, the crossbar is being raised! As good as I was getting, there was always so much better that I could be.

Given my misguided concept about God, I don't really know what compelled me to go to church. Perhaps it was my mother's prayers for me. Whatever it was that drew me to

Seeking to be holy is a little like being a high jumper. You clear one height, and the next thing you know, the crossbar is being raised!

church, I went every Sunday, even though I had to walk about a mile to get there during most of my older childhood and young teen years. My mother went sometimes, but on many Sundays, she sent me on my own.

I always sat on the end of the second row, right in front of the pulpit. I listened very intently. The pastor, to me, seemed ancient, and he talked slowly. But for some reason, I was always intensely interested in what he was saying.

When I was about nine years old—and again when I was twelve—my grandfather invited me to spend a week with him in North Carolina. He was preaching a revival that week. My grandfather was a tall, lanky fellow, and hearing and watching him preach, I felt as if I were hearing God Himself speak. I remember kneeling down and praying between the pews of that church where the revival was being held. It was a Pentecostal church, and the Pentecostals there prayed loud and long.

Later in my twelfth year, I went to church one morning, and Mrs. Wilson was preaching a revival at our church. I was standing in the second row, my usual spot, and I knew that when she gave the altar call, I just had to go forward. I fell on my knees, and before I knew it, five of my Sunday school friends had knelt with me and were praying for me. I cried and prayed and asked the Lord to save me, and I told Him that I believed in Jesus and His death and resurrection.

The pastor asked me to come up and tell the people what the Lord had done for me. I remember standing behind that pulpit and saying, "I don't know everything He's done for me, but I know He's saved me." I knew it without any doubt.

It was an experience that changed my life, even though it altered very little my understanding of God's accessibility.

My mother was not there that Sunday morning, but I told her what had happened when I returned home, and she thought it was wonderful. I also told some of my friends, but they weren't interested. From the very beginning, my salvation experience was something I experienced alone, and my faith walk was also something I was required to walk alone—except, of course, for the presence of Jesus Christ.

I made the time that I delivered my newspapers my prayer time. I had a real sense that Jesus heard me when I talked to Him about things that were happening in my life, at school, at home, with my friends and Mom. Jesus was very real to me. God the Father remained farther away, dwelling in a distant somewhere. I had no concept or feeling that God could be close to me. I was saved, but I still felt unworthy of that kind of intimacy with the Lord.

THE MISSING MESSAGE OF GRACE

In looking back over the years, I have come to realize that I heard woefully few sermons about the grace of God in all those Sundays at church. Actually, I've heard relatively few sermons on grace since then! It's my firm opinion that most pastors preach far more about works than grace. I'd say more than 90 percent of their sermons are related to the need for us to line up with God's rules.

Many preachers may say they are preaching salvation on a regular basis, but most of those who say that are really preaching repentance. They are requiring that people do something *first* before God can extend Himself to them.

The truth is that God is extending Himself toward us continually and in more ways than can be counted. He is forever offering Himself to us. He doesn't forgive us because we call up our sins (which God already knows), recount our misdoings, or beg and plead in repentance. All we really need to do is to accept and receive what God has already given to us—the free gift of salvation, free grace, and the freedom to enter God's presence.

Your salvation—and mine—is based on the answer to one question and one question alone: "Am I willing by faith to receive Jesus Christ as my personal Savior based on the fact that when He died on Calvary, He paid my sin debt in full?"

If I say yes to that question, I am receiving Christ into my life. When I receive Him, I am receiving Him by faith. I believe in Him as my personal Savior.

Repentance, on the other hand, is something I do by my will because of what God does in my heart when I receive Him by faith. I turn away from sin because something has happened in my heart, not so that something will happen in my heart. We repent as the result of accepting Jesus and experiencing His grace at work in us.

Accepting Jesus is as simple as accepting Him as your Savior and accepting that what He did is sufficient to establish your relationship with God.

Let me state it yet another way. The only thing that is

I turn away from sin because something has happened in my heart, not so that something will happen in my heart.

required for you to receive Jesus Christ as your Savior is to believe that He is the Son of God, that He died on the cross to pay your sin debt, that He is your Savior and Lord.

To put anything else on people as a requirement for their salvation is to burden them with works and diminish the grace of God at work in their lives.

Romans 10:9–10 tells us plainly, "If you confess with your mouth the Lord Jesus and believe in your heart that God has raised Him from the dead, you will be saved. For with the heart one believes unto righteousness, and with the mouth confession is made unto salvation."

This understanding of grace, which I gained just a few years ago, has totally transformed the way I preach. Once people understand that they don't need to change before they come to God, that they don't need to plead and beg God to accept them, and that God's grace is extended to them and all they need to do is accept it by faith and believe in Jesus, they experience a tremendous transformation in their lives. I'm seeing people become set free from

◆ feeling a need to get God's approval.

◆ performing for God.

◆ experiencing guilt over not doing enough for God or being good enough for God.

The apostle Paul asked, "Shall we continue in sin that grace may abound?" and then he answered his own question, "Certainly not!" (Rom. 6:1–2). Their desire for sin is greatly diminished. Once a person has experienced God's free gift of grace, she desires to fall on her face and cry out to God and praise Him and worship Him. She doesn't want to go out and sin.

Once a person really understands the fullness and the extent of God's grace toward him, you can't keep him from accepting the Lord! Such a person can hardly wait to be in relationship with God.

When we think that we have to get good enough to get God, that we have to do something to gain God's favor, or that we need to make changes in our lives before we can get saved, we are reluctant to make the effort, probably out of fear that even if we make the effort, it won't be sufficient.

WHAT DO WE DO WHEN WE SIN?

As a Christian, you may be saying at this point, "I still sin. I don't want to sin. But I still do."

Don't be dismayed. We are all in that same boat. Even Paul admitted, "I do what I don't want to do, and I don't do what I want to do." (See Rom. 7:19.)

The prayer in those times must become, "God, I'm struggling. I'm not doing well. I'm failing. Please forgive me and help me." I may not get a quick answer or immediate relief from the thing I'm struggling with, but I know that forgiveness by God is instantaneous. My understanding about what to do may take time—in fact, it usually does take time because it's a process of growth—but when it comes to forgiveness, I know that forgiveness is granted the moment I request it.

My forgiveness was resolved on the cross nearly two thousand years ago. I don't need to plead and beg for God to forgive me. I simply need to ask God to forgive me and then accept the fact that He has and He does.

I see many Christians who beg and beg for forgiveness, day in and day out. They need to understand that God heard their request the first time they uttered it! Once they have repented of sins and received God's forgiveness initially in their lives, they come to the Father as forgiven children.

When forgiven people sin and ask God's forgiveness, they actually ask God's forgiveness so that their relationship with God might be strengthened and their fellowship with God might be renewed. They ask God to remove that thing inhibiting the growing, warm, and intimate fellowship with the Lord. They do not ask for forgiveness to reestablish fellowship.

LETTING GO OF THE PAST

In the course of my ministry, I have met countless people who are haunted by their sins. They have not been able to forgive themselves and let go of their past.

The Bible tells us that once we have repented of our sins, God both forgives them and forgets them. Listen to the words of the Lord in Isaiah 43:25:

> I, even I, am He who blots out
> your transgressions for My own sake;
> And I will not remember your sins.

It is not the Lord, therefore, who reminds you of past sins that you have already confessed to Him. God would never haunt you about something for which He has forgiven you. He won't bring to your remembrance something He has forgotten! Such haunting memories are inspired from the enemy of your soul, the devil. When you are confronted with images or memories of sins you have already confessed to God, it's time to say, "I refuse to accept these thoughts. God has already forgiven me of that. I'm letting this go right on by. Devil, you'll have no hold on my mind."

ACCEPTING GOD'S TRANSFORMING POWER

Others are convinced that they have an uncontrollable ability to sin or a propensity to sin in a certain area. When people begin to think that way about themselves and they conclude that they have no ability to withstand temptation, they are really putting themselves in a weakened position. They are setting themselves up mentally and emotionally to sin again because they are anticipating and expecting to sin— as opposed to anticipating that the Lord will help them overcome temptation. The expectation must be an expectation not to sin.

If you feel that you are weak in a particular area, it's time to say, "Lord, I want to thank You that You are my strength, my resistance, my power. Your grace is superabounding. Lord, You have said that no matter what sin I face, You have more power to help me withstand that temptation than the devil has power to tempt. I'm putting my trust in You to release Your life in me."

Focus on the Lord's provision to keep you from sinning

rather than on the sin or on your weakness. The Bible tells us, "Make no provision for the flesh, to fulfill its lusts" (Rom. 13:14). In other words, don't expect your lusts and your flesh to win out over your spirit. Don't make excuses for your sinful desires or attempt to justify your sinful behavior as something you just can't control. In so doing, you are mentally, emotionally, and spiritually laying the foundation for another failure.

Rather than turn your attention to the thing that is tempting you, turn your attention immediately to the Lord. Think upon Him, put your thoughts on His Word, and turn your attention to those things that are true, noble, just, pure, lovely, and of good report (see Phil. 4:8).

Never assume that God made you to sin. Many people attempt to justify their sin by saying, "Well, God just made me that way." No, He did not. God created you in His image with a free will, with which you decide your actions and your responses to life. God's desire is that you not sin—rather, that you live a life of righteousness before Him so that He can bless you fully with every good thing He has planned and prepared for you.

SINS AND MISTAKES ARE DIFFERENT

I have asked myself a number of times, "Would I have changed any major decision in my life?" And the answer is no.

That isn't to say I haven't made some bad decisions or made mistakes. But I know that God has worked those bad decisions for good, and that when the time came for the major decisions in my life, God revealed Himself so clearly that I was able to make the right decision.

Let me make a clear distinction between a sin and a mistake. Many people get them confused, and as a result, they live in a spirit of condemnation and guilt that is totally unnecessary.

Briefly stated, a sin is a choice to do something that we know is against God's will. A sin is a willful act—one that is calculated, thought out, anticipated, and fully conscious. A sin is deliberate. It is flying in the face of what we know is right in God's eyes.

A mistake is usually spur of the moment, unplanned, and made without forethought of consequences. A mistake is a miscalculation, an error in judgment (frequently based on an error in research or information received).

What are we to do about our mistakes?

First, we can own up to our mistakes and learn from them. For example, I know in looking back that I have made errors in the hiring of several staff members. I looked at all the external factors related to the person—the person was knowledgeable, would be loyal, had all the right degrees, and had a good track record. The people I hired had all the potential in the world. And yet they didn't work out.

What caused me to make a mistake?

I have come to recognize that I made those mistakes out of a feeling of personal desperation—a feeling that I needed somebody right away. I let my decision to hire a person be driven by my need rather than by God's desire.

Personal need and desperation are never good reasons to

make decisions. Those motivations can often lead to unwise decisions.

I also came to realize that I make much wiser decisions about staff when I refuse to trust solely my judgment. I never hire a staff member now without consensus from other members of the staff.

I've learned, and I'm still learning, from mistakes.

Second, we can turn to the Lord when we make mistakes and entrust them to Him. We can ask Him to turn a situation around, to make right what has gone wrong, and to cause good to come from our mistakes.

My wife, Annie, and I experienced a very practical example of this in our lives when we first moved to Atlanta. We had been in the city several months and were feeling very pressed to make a decision and get settled. We found a house that wasn't totally what we were looking for, but in a number of ways it seemed adequate, so we put a deposit on the house. One requirement we wrote into the contract was that the house have a dry basement.

The day after we had put the deposit on the house, we found the house that we really wanted. We felt as if we had found *our* house, but we were already committed to the other one.

I said, "We probably acted out of our discouragement. We'll just have to ask God to deal with this for us." We got down on our knees and prayed about it.

That night Atlanta experienced its biggest rainstorm in twenty years. The basement of the house on which we had put a deposit flooded, and we were released from our contract.

We had made a mistake. We had prayed about a house, we had hunted for a house on a daily basis, but when it came to making a decision, we had acted one step ahead of God. We had let our discouragement and our need for a house force us into action rather than wait for the precise answer to our prayers. And yet, even though we made a mistake, God knew that our desire was to have the house of His choice, and He provided for it.

Entrust your mistakes to God. He can fix them far better than you can.

ARE YOU FEELING AS IF YOU HAVE MISSED GOD?

You may feel today as if you've missed something that God wanted you to do—that He called you to do something for Him and you failed to do it.

Ask yourself, "Was that call really of God, or was it something of my desire? Was it a true call, or was it my personal daydream or wish at the time? Was it something God wanted me to do or something someone else thought I should do?"

If the call was not really from God, God does not hold you responsible for what you thought was His plan for you.

You may say, "But how can I tell if the call was truly a call or if it was my desire at the time?"

Ask yourself, "Was there ever a time when I was confronted with an opportunity to act on that call, and I said no?" For example, you may have walked forward during a missionary conference one time and committed your life to work for God as a missionary. That's not the same as God saying to you, "I want you to accept this invitation to travel to Africa and be My representative in this particular city." The former commitment is a general commitment to do God's will should He call you to go. The latter example is an acceptance of God's specific order for you to *act* on a call. If the opportunity has never presented itself in a concrete, specific way for you to go overseas as a missionary, don't be troubled with feelings of guilt that you've failed God. You haven't!

In some cases, of course, you may say, "But I did say no when God told me to do something very specific." If that's the case, now is the time to turn to the Lord and say, "Lord, I'm sorry I disobeyed You. I ask You to forgive me. I put myself before You today. Whatever You want me to do, I'll do it." Listen for what the Lord tells you to do next, and then obey Him and follow through.

If **you assume that because you have failed God once—or even more than once—in the past, He will never use you in the future, you are limiting God.**

✳

If you assume that because you have failed God once— or even more than once—in the past, He will never use you in the future, you are limiting God. God has the ability to forgive. He has the ability to turn your failures into triumphs. He is able to figure out a place that's just right for your particular talents and gifts. And furthermore, He desires to put you to use in His kingdom.

You may say, "Well, I didn't refuse a call from God, but I sinned in a major way. God will never be able to use me."

Again, you are limiting the ability of God. God can heal your life, restore you, put you back together, put you back on track with Him, and use you. Trust Him to do it!

Just look at the number of people who have been to

prison, failed miserably, fallen from grace (I do not mean they lost their salvation), suffered great disrepute or a loss of reputation, and God has lifted them up and restored them. Very often, the latter days of their lives are more fruitful for Him than their former days before the failure.

I believe that you can misread, misjudge, and make a mistake, but if the desire of your heart is to do God's will, God will find a way to turn your mistake around and lead you into the right path.

In 1984, I was 100 percent convinced in my heart that I would not be chosen as president of the Southern Baptist Convention. It was not something I wanted. I didn't believe it was God's plan for my life.

The night before the nominations were made, I was in a prayer meeting with a group of people who had gathered to pray about and to discuss the nomination for president.

Bertha Smith, a missionary to China for more than forty years and a woman who probably did more to get Southern Baptist pastors attuned to the Holy Spirit than anybody else, was in that prayer meeting. She felt as if I was the one to be nominated, and she said to me, "Charles, you need to get down on your knees and repent and get right with God." I did what she told me, of course! But I still went away from that meeting with a fairly clear idea about who was going to be nominated—and it wasn't me. The fact was, I felt quite good about that other person receiving the nomination.

The next morning as I prepared to leave our hotel room for the convention meetings, I reached for the knob on the door of our room, and the Lord spoke in my heart, *Don't put your hand on that doorknob unless you are willing to do what I tell you.* I broke out crying.

I've discovered over the years that every time God brings me to a crucial moment in my life, I burst out in tears for no explainable reason. I seem to go from no emotion to overwhelming emotion in a moment's time when God gives me an insight into what He's calling me to do.

I began to pray, and the Lord confirmed to me that I needed to be willing to be nominated, even if I lost and was humiliated in the process. After more than a little soul-searching and struggle, I finally said, "Okay, God." I left my hotel room and went back to the place where we had been meeting in prayer the night before, and I found a number of the people still there. They had been praying all night.

The man I had felt certain would be nominated came to me and said, "I'm not going to do it." I told the group what had happened to me, and they began to rejoice and praise God. Several said, "We knew it all along. We were just waiting for you to agree."

Now, after all the hurt, turmoil, trials, and tribulations that arose from that convention, I may well have asked myself, "Was I wrong?" One thing I know for sure is that when I face God, I will have done what I really believed with all of my heart was the right thing. From God's vantage point or in the opinion of other people, it may have been the wrong thing, but I have no personal conviction of that in my heart. To the best of my awareness, I have done what God has asked me to do.

I don't want to ever find myself questioning with regret, "I wonder what God would have done if I had said yes to what I felt was His leading at the time?" I have an assurance in my heart that I have obeyed God to the best of my ability, and that my heart's desire has always been to obey Him. If I have erred, I have to trust God that He will make it right and create a way for me to understand Him better and to do His will even more perfectly in the future.

God knows our human frailties. He knows how to overcome them and how to work through them, around them, and in them. God knows how to fix our mistakes.

The Bible tells us that the Lord looks at our hearts—our motives, our desires, our innermost thoughts—not our achievements. He judges us on our faithfulness, not our success.

God knows our human frailties. God knows how to fix our mistakes.

ONLY YOU KNOW FOR SURE

You, and only you, know today if you are right with God. If you aren't, you can be. There's nothing you have done, and nothing you are, that is beyond God's love for you. He stands ready to forgive you and to receive you fully into His presence, to adopt you as His child, and to be present with you every moment of the rest of your life.

You, and only you, know today if you are following God's plan for your life. If you aren't, you can start anew right now. God has a plan for you that He's just waiting to put into effect.

You, and only you, know today if you are carrying the excess emotional baggage of guilt. If you are, you can be free of that guilt. You can accept the definitive work of Jesus

Christ on the cross, be transformed, and become a new spiritual creation. You can accept the fact that once you are forgiven, you are in a growth process of transformation. You can ask God to take your mistakes and your errors—the stumbling-stones of your life—and turn them into stepping-stones.

The Lord's desire for you today is that you be free of guilt and sin. All you need to do is to take Him up on His offer to carry the load of your guilt and sin for you.

TRUTH CAPSULE

When you are struggling under the weight of guilt and sin . . .

1. Accept Jesus as your Savior from sin. Receive what He has done for you and what He desires to give you—His very presence that will free you, empower you, and cause you to be transformed into a person who is pure, holy, and completely cleansed in your soul.

2. Follow Jesus as your Lord. Ask for His help in living out your life. Give Him your mistakes, and ask Him to turn them toward good.

3. Acknowledge Jesus as your way. He said of Himself, "I am the way, the truth, and the life" (John 14:6). Trust Him to show you His path and to give you the courage to walk in it.

My excess baggage from guilt.

_____
_____
_____
_____
_____
_____
_____
_____
_____

How I can lighten this load.

_____
_____
_____
_____
_____
_____
_____
_____
_____

God is the source of my strength.

Words
of
comfort
and
healing
to
those
who
are

6

FRUSTRATED

My best friend in high school was a fellow by the name of Raymond. He was a Baptist, and I was in the Holiness church at the time. One evening when we were both fourteen years old, we were sitting out in a ball field, and I asked Raymond, "What are you going to do when you grow up?"

He said, "I don't know. What are you going to do?"

I said, "I don't know."

We later confessed to each other that we both knew that we were going to preach, but we were too scared to admit it.

There was never a time when I felt God say directly to me, *I want you to preach.* But from the time I was saved, I never really thought about doing anything else. Preaching just always seemed to me to be what I was destined to do.

*N*ot understanding at that time how God's transforming grace works in a person's life, I did what just about any person with my emotional baggage would do: I drove myself to be the most perfect pastor who had ever lived. ◆

Since I came to adulthood with a heavy load of emotional baggage—little self-esteem, lots of insecurities, a life-long experience of loneliness—being a pastor was probably one of the least likely things I should have aspired to do.

Being a pastor meant dealing with lots of people. I had virtually no experience with that. Being a pastor meant holding a public position of leadership. Again, there was nothing in my background to prepare me for assuming that role.

Not understanding at that time how God's transforming grace works in a person's life, I did what just about any person with my emotional baggage would do: I drove myself to be the most perfect pastor who had ever lived. I studied long and hard, and I prayed long and hard. I did everything in my power to do the very best I could.

Now, trying hard to do one's best isn't wrong. But my motive was wrong.

I didn't realize it, but I was trying to gain God's acceptance; I was attempting to get Him to love me and to approve of me—in some fashion, in some way. Deep down inside, you see, I thought that I was unlovable, and that I needed to improve myself and be perfect so that God would find me lovable.

As a perfectionist, you never know when you are measuring up to God's expectations, and therefore, you never know when you are good enough to get God's approval.

✳

As I discussed in an earlier chapter, one of the problems with being a perfectionist is that you never know when you are measuring up to God's expectations, and therefore, you never know when you are good enough to get God's approval. I was on a quest that had no definable end, but I didn't know that at the time. I plunged headlong toward an impossible goal.

I didn't just try hard—I drove myself. And not only that, I drove other people. My wife once said to me, "You don't get ulcers. You give them to the people around you." That was probably very true. The person who drives himself cannot stand laziness or slothfulness in himself or in anybody else. The perfectionist's attitude is one of doing all that you can do, and then doing a little bit more. It's an attitude governed by shoulds and oughts—"I should do this; I ought to do that." Shoulds and oughts governed just about everything I did for many years.

I didn't want God's approval alone, of course. I also wanted the approval of those who called me their pastor.

I feel sure that I stood at the door on many a Sunday morning after I had preached primarily in hopes of hearing someone say, "That was a wonderful sermon. I really appreciated that." Or "That was so good . . . you so blessed me." I felt a desperate need for approval to try to compensate for the years of rejection and disapproval I had known.

Three other aspects of the perfectionist attitude of striving are worth noting. I had them all:

◆ *Control.* I was very uneasy unless I was in charge. No matter what was happening, I felt I had to be in control.

◆ *Combativeness.* No matter what was going on, I was ready to fight if somebody wanted to fight. I was a very competitive person. That, no doubt, stemmed in part from my survival spirit of do or die. When a person is a perfectionist, he does whatever is necessary to win and to be the best. It doesn't make any difference what area of life is involved, a perfectionist doesn't quit, never says die, and keeps doing whatever he thinks is necessary to reach the top or be the best.

◆ *Criticism.* I had a very critical spirit. If a person didn't live up to my standard—which would have been very difficult to define and always impossible to reach—I was critical. A perfectionist is critical of everybody all the time.

The problem, of course, is that no matter how much

you want to be in control, there are always circumstances or people that won't cooperate.

No matter how much you push those around you to be perfect, they never are.

Fighting only puts people on the defensive and eventually drives them away.

And criticizing those who fail to meet your standards generally causes them to continue to fail.

The result is that the striving perfectionist achieves only one thing: constant irritation and frustration.

IRRITATION AND FRUSTRATION ARE INSIDE JOBS

Irritation and frustration are inner events. They are rooted in a person's emotional health.

People often blame external circumstances and situations for the irritation they feel, but the external things of life don't cause irritation—they simply trigger what is already inside a person.

Anyone who is feeling irritated and frustrated all the time needs to face squarely what it is deep within that is causing that response to life. There's something that the person

◆ hasn't dealt with.
◆ is running from.
◆ hasn't identified.
◆ won't recognize.
◆ is totally ignorant of.

◆ refuses to face.

The comments we pastors and counselors hear cover a wide range of frustrations: "Nothing seems to be going right"; "Interruptions, interruptions, interruptions. I can't seem to get anything done"; "I feel as if I'm going in circles at ninety miles an hour and getting nowhere"; "I'd do just fine if he'd stop behaving the way he does."

Very often there's a prevailing attitude of, "I'm right. It's everyone else who is wrong." The reality, however, is that everybody else can't be wrong all of the time in every situation. What's wrong is on the inside of the person who thinks that's the case!

Once you have identified what is truly at the core of your irritation and frustration, you must deal with it.

Very often, frustration and irritation are rooted in

◆ an inability to accept the way God has created the person.

◆ a reluctance to face a problem in the past.

◆ a refusal to confront something that the person knows is wrong and contrary to God's purposes and plan.

Ask yourself if you feel a constant sense of irritability or frustration: "Am I a striver? Do I always feel as if I have to win? Do I always feel that I've failed if I don't get an *A*, don't win the top prize, or don't come in first?"

Many people take their drive to excel into their relationship with Christ. They seek to be number one in everything they do for the Lord. They desire to be the best Christian who ever lived.

As I stated earlier, God doesn't compare people— whether Christian to non-Christian, or Christian to Christian.

He doesn't rank people in percentiles or give out rewards based on firsts, mosts, or bests.

The Christian who is striving to be the best Christian on the earth needs to ask, "Why am I striving so hard? What am I expecting to get or earn?"

Is it a matter of pride—that you desire to be recognized over your peers or competitors?

Is it a matter of control—that you are seeking to gain power out of your achievements?

Is it a matter of inadequacy—that you still believe you must do more in order for God, or another person, to approve of you or love you?

Let me share some good news with you.

God couldn't possibly love you more than He loves you right now. God couldn't possibly approve of you more than He does today.

You are His child, and He loves you just the way you are —right now. He knows that you are in the process of becoming, but He also takes responsibility for what you will become and how fast you will become it. He says to you, "Let Me do the striving on your behalf! Let Me do the work in you. All you have to do is receive what I want to do in you and through you. Accept My offer. Let Me do the perfecting work."

A GOD-GIVEN SENSE OF FRUSTRATION

There are times when a sense of irritability is not rooted in your sense of failure, inadequacy, or desire for perfection, but a sense of frustration is placed in your spirit by God.

This type of frustration can be differentiated by four qualities:

1. You are not trying to beat or conquer anybody or anything.
2. The onset of the frustration is usually quite sudden and intense—and even upon careful inner evaluation, there doesn't seem to be a cause for it.
3. The frustration is not with anybody else but with yourself alone.
4. Once you move into the new path that God is leading you to walk, the frustration ends.

When that type of frustration manifests itself in your life, rejoice! God is plowing up your soul and forcing you to confront and face a deeper part of your character. God is seeking to forgive, resolve, or transform a new area of your life. He is stirring you up, keeping you agitated until you face your problem, your sin, your error, your very nature. He won't let you be at peace until you face yourself squarely, but once you do, you'll find that the Lord is doing a work in you that is for your growth and, ultimately, your eternal good.

God uses our growth out of pain to make us more effective in our faith. Such growth brings us to a higher point of service. It conforms us into the likeness of Jesus Christ so

Rejoice! God is plowing up your soul and forcing you to confront and face a deeper part of your character.

that we will truly become the people that He desires to live with forever.

Romans 8:28 tells us, "We know that all things work together for good to those who love God, to those who are the called according to His purpose." The next two verses go on to tell us God's purpose in working everything together for our good—so that we might be transformed into the likeness of Jesus Christ: "For whom He foreknew, He also predestined to be conformed to the image of His Son, that He might be the firstborn among many brethren. Moreover whom He predestined, these He also called; whom He called, these He also justified; and whom He justified, these He also glorified" (Rom. 8:29–30).

When you have a churning feeling deep inside you—a restlessness in your soul—that can be one of the most exciting times of your life. God is at work in you; He's about to move into a deeper, more fulfilling experience in your walk with Him.

That's the time when you need to do several things.

First, make sure that everything is right between you and God. Face up to any sins that the Lord reveals to you, ask God's forgiveness, and then make a decision with your will to change your past ways. Ask the Lord to prepare you for what He has in store for you. Read God's Word with renewed vigor, always on the alert for verses that God may cause to leap off the page as you read them.

Second, start *expecting* God to show you what He is leading you to do. Wait in eager anticipation for God to reveal your next move. Thank the Lord for getting you ready to take the next step, for giving you a new challenge or opportunity.

It's important that you recognize that this type of expectancy is far different from feelings of inner compulsion or obsession.

Compulsions and obsessions are frequently the outcropping of perfectionism. They are a trap, not a blessing. They are rooted in a drive to have something you do not have or to gain something you have not gained. A key question to ask yourself is, "When I get what I want, will I really want what I get?"

Many times people drive themselves to achieve something—or to acquire something—that really doesn't satisfy their inner longing once they have achieved it or acquired it.

Obsessions and greed are very often closely linked. The more people want, the more there is to want. The more people have, the more they realize what they don't have. In obsessions, the more people strive to have control over something, the more they usually realize that they can never have total control over it because, ultimately, they don't have control over themselves!

The only things in life that truly satisfy are the things that are intangible and that only God can give us. Stop to think for a moment about what you truly value in life. On your list will no doubt be these items:

- A long, fruitful, and fulfilled life
- Good health
- A loving circle of family and friends
- The hope of eternal life
- Inner peace and joy

Not one of these things can you acquire on your own. Each is something that, in the final analysis, only God can provide. You can take certain actions that will enhance your ability to have these things, but you can never fully acquire them on your own.

Things other than what God alone can provide are just that—things. They never satisfy. They always disappoint—they break, rust, get stolen, get lost, lose value, decay, rot, or tarnish. They don't last.

Third, start evaluating what you *don't* want in your life, *don't* want out of life, and *don't* want to do or be in life.

Very often the Lord leads us into His will by giving us a great distaste for what isn't His will. Our sins and sinful nature become abhorrent to us. Things we once craved we no longer can tolerate. People we once admired we no longer place on a pedestal. Places we once frequented we never desire to enter again. Habits we once had slough away. Goals we once set no longer seem important.

I knew early in my preparation to be a preacher what I didn't want to be like. It seemed to me that the more preachers I met, the more I found men who were administrators and not really very spiritual men.

While in seminary, I did meet one man who wasn't like the norm. I was given an old-fashioned wire recording of a sermon by Dr. W. A. Criswell. I said to myself, "I've got to hear this man in person." Annie and I drove over to his church in Dallas on a Saturday night—about thirty miles from where we were studying in Fort Worth—because I wanted to go to a service there the next night and I wanted to be sure I knew the way. We walked into First Baptist Church in Dallas on Saturday evening, and I was stunned. I had never been in a church that big in all my life. We looked around and spent some time praying there. And then the next evening, we drove back over for a service.

I had never seen Dr. Criswell before that night, but when he stood up in the pulpit and opened his Bible to Romans 5:1–2 and began to preach, "This grace wherein we stand," excitement filled me. I knew that I had found someone who preached the way I had only dreamed preaching could be. Dr. Criswell was as much or more a motivator and a role model for me than anyone I encountered at seminary. I saw in him a man who was into the Word and who preached with enthusiasm.

Dr. Criswell stood in sharp contrast to most of my professors in seminary—some I felt were very noncommittal about the gospel, and others seemed more intent on pouring us seminarians into a mold. Overall, I felt very restless and spiritually frustrated in seminary. I was continually trying to sort out what I believed. Much of the time, I was concluding what I didn't believe.

An inner God-given restlessness and spiritual frustration can bring you to a place of re-sorting your priorities in life and of chopping away at those things that are extraneous, unimportant, or not in God's will for you.

Fourth, when you experience a restlessness in your spirit, look for the Lord to give you strong impressions—or checks —in your spirit to guide you into His path.

A God-given restlessness or spiritual frustration very often manifests itself as a strong impression of "this is right to do," "this period or phase is over," "now is the time to move," or "here's the next move." I've experienced a number of manifestations of this in my spirit during the course of my ministry. Each time the Lord has dealt with me in a little different way, but the overall pattern has been one of a churning within that didn't end until I had prayed and made the decision that was right in the Lord's eyes. I first experienced this God-given restlessness while we were in seminary.

As I faced the prospect of graduating from seminary, I didn't know where to turn. I didn't have a clue about how to get a church to pastor, and I didn't know anybody who could or would recommend me to a church. I also felt that if I had to be recommended, something must be wrong. My constant prayer was, "Lord, I trust You."

At the end of our second year at seminary, Annie and I decided to spend the summer working for the home missions board in California—I planned to preach and Annie to sing. On a Saturday morning, we began praying together about the summer, and we became so burdened that we prayed all day long. By the end of the day, we had concluded that God didn't want us to go to California. But what then?

Annie's father had given her a very fine cottage up on Lake Lure in Hickory Nut Gorge, North Carolina. Since we didn't have any definite plans, we went up there to spend the summer relaxing. After four years of working and studying in college, and then two years of seminary, I really appreciated a couple of months to rest.

The last month we were there, we were out fishing one day, and a man called out to me from the dock. He said that his pastor was going to be gone for two weeks, and he asked if I would preach for his church. I said, "Sure I will." I hadn't preached that much, and I felt inadequate as a preacher. But that day, I felt compelled to say yes without hesitation to his invitation.

The next Sunday I went to the village of Fruitland, near Hendersonville, and preached. The following Sunday, the pastor was present for the services, and after the evening meeting, a group including the pastor met with us. The pastor, Noah Abraham Melton, had been there forty-seven years, and that night he told me that he was preparing to retire and that the group wanted me to be the next pastor.

I said, "I've still got a year of seminary left."

They said, "We'll wait for you."

I said, "No, you don't want to do that."

The pastor spoke up, "We're going to build a brand-new house for the next pastor so you go on back to school for a year. We're willing to wait, and we'll get the house built by then."

I said, "Well, I'll have to think and pray about that." In a couple of weeks, we returned to seminary. A short time later we received a letter from the church saying that the members had voted unanimously for me to be their pastor.

At that time in my life, I had very little information about the Baptists, and I had no interest whatsoever in denominations as a whole. I just wanted to preach the gospel.

My association with the Baptist church had started when I was about fifteen years old. I began dating a Baptist girl and attending church with her on Sunday nights. About that same time, the pastor retired at the Pentecostal church I had been attending. I asked my mother what she thought about the possibility of my joining the Baptist church, and she said, "If you can live just as holy a life in the Baptist church as in the Pentecostal Holiness church, that's all right with me." I had to think about her statement awhile. In my view at that time, being in the Pentecostal Holiness church was about as holy as a person could get. By comparison, being in the Baptist church was almost like backsliding.

My Sunday school teacher at the Baptist church was a big cigar-smoking real estate agent. The lessons were sometimes so bad I walked out. In contrast, the pastor, Reverend Hammock, really preached the Bible. He was a great soul winner and a genuinely fine man. Eventually, Pastor Hammock's example won out, and I joined.

To have attended the Baptist church in high school and college was one thing. My real commitment had never been to the church. It was to Jesus Christ. To become a Baptist pastor was to make a much more serious commitment to the Baptist denomination. We prayed a long time before we concluded that we were willing to accept the call.

In addition to the call from the church at Fruitland, I received a call from the president of the Fruitland Baptist Bible Institute where Pastor Melton had taught, and he asked me if I was willing to teach homiletics, preaching, and evangelism in the institute. Each of the 160 students enrolled at the institute was ordained, older than I, and a pastor with experience. I thought, *God, what's going on?* At the same time, I felt impressed that it was what God wanted me to do.

One day while browsing in a bookstore close to the seminary, I found a book by R. A. Torrey, *The Holy Spirit— Who He Is and What He Does*. I didn't feel as if I had enough money to buy the book so I'd go into the bookstore and read a few pages, put the book back on the shelf, come back another day, read a few more pages, and then put the book back again. That went on for a while until I decided I had to have the book. I devoured it.

When I'd bring up the subject of the Holy Spirit in my theology class, however, I was so ridiculed that I finally made an appointment to see my theology professor. I said, "I want to talk about the Holy Spirit."

He responded, "When you got saved, you got all there is."

I said, "Well, I've got to have a better answer than that." We had a big argument, and I finally said to myself, *Lord, I've just got to trust You.*

I believed vitally in my need to be filled with the Holy Spirit and to have some kind of anointing from God to do the job that lay ahead of me. September was on the horizon. I was going to be called upon to be a pastor, to preach regularly, and to teach three courses to students I felt probably knew as much or more about the subjects than I did! A deep restlessness filled my heart for more of God.

We moved to Fruitland after I graduated in May. I was to begin teaching in the Bible School the following fall. I knew I wasn't ready; there was something missing.

I prayed and studied and prayed and studied night and day all summer. My spiritual frustration only grew. On the Friday before the classes at the institute were to start on Monday, I had reached the desperation point. I said to the Lord, "God, I've got to be filled with the Holy Spirit. Whatever it takes! I've been praying all summer long, and I can't face Monday morning without the Holy Spirit!"

About four o'clock in the afternoon, I had I John 5:14–15 opened before me as I was kneeling on the rug in my study, and I said to the Lord, "God, I've done everything I know to do. I've prayed and fasted and cried, and the only thing I know to do is to claim what You said—'Now this is the confidence that we have in Him, that if we ask anything according to His will, He hears us. And if we know that He hears us, whatever we ask, we know that we have the petitions that we have asked of Him.' " And I know that in that hour, on that old rug in my office, God filled me with the Holy Spirit. I said to Annie, "I know something has happened to me!" God had satisfied the restlessness in my heart in a definitive way.

I walked into my first class with confidence. I knew that I was ready. I felt without doubt that Someone was inside me, and He was going to work through me. I wasn't afraid of anything or anybody. And the students accepted me instantly. We had a great year, and the Spirit began to move in a new way in the school.

I was at Fruitland for two years, and I loved every day of our stay there. I prayed and studied and preached and taught day and night. All I did was pray, study, preach, and teach. What little time I had for recreation, we hunted in the mountains and fished in the lake.

One day while driving back from Hendersonville, about a hundred yards before I got to the bridge on the Fruitland Road, I knew beyond a shadow of a doubt that my time in Fruitland was over. It was an entirely different way of the Lord's dealing with me. It was as if an intense feeling overcame me, and with it, all of my burden and love for Fruitland disappeared. The feeling was sudden, unexpected—the very thought of leaving Fruitland had not crossed my mind before that moment.

On Sunday morning, a pulpit committee from Fairborne, Ohio, visited my church. I had been referred to them by the executive secretary of the Ohio Baptist convention, who had come to Fruitland to preach at one of our spiritual emphasis weeks.

I didn't know the committee was there that Sunday, but a few days later, we received an invitation to go to Ohio. Given my experience on the Fruitland Road, I felt I had to at least take a look. I didn't want to go, but I felt I had to go. And ultimately, I felt God leading us to accept the invitation.

The time we spent in Ohio was like a wilderness experience for me. The area was flat, with few trees, and it seemed too cold in the winter, too hot in the summer. I did meet a lot of young pastors about my age there, and we had good fellowship. It was a pioneer area for the Southern Baptists, but I was ready to leave when the time came. Once again, the Lord worked in a unique way. There was no period of restlessness, no advance feeling that we were to leave, no sense of ending to the time in Fairborne.

I was invited to be part of a group of pastors who were asked to preach for two weeks in Haiti. On the way to Haiti, I stopped in Miami and preached at a church there at the invitation of a friend of mine who had a cabin in the Fruitland area. My uncle Jack came to visit the church that morning. He was not a Christian at the time and had never heard me preach before, so I preached my heart out to him for forty-five minutes. The result was that the church called me to be the pastor. Again, I wasn't sure at first, but as we prayed, the more we felt that the idea of moving to Miami was God's idea and that He had arranged the circumstances that led us there. We felt a strong assurance that it was God's next move for us.

We absolutely loved every minute of our years in Miami. In many ways, we felt as if we had died and gone to heaven. The church prospered and grew. We were close to the beach and a block from our children's school. We went camping and fishing as a family. After being there for three years, however, I began to feel a restlessness in my spirit. I knew the Lord was plowing me up about something, but I didn't know what it was. I fasted and prayed often, trying to discern what the Lord was trying to teach me. It never dawned on me at the time that the restlessness in my heart meant another move. That was the farthest thing from my mind. Rather, I assumed that the frustration I was feeling had to do with a sermon series that the Lord wanted me to preach but that I hadn't yet discerned.

I was preaching on the book of Galatians at the time, and I was coming up on the fifth chapter, which is about the fruit of the Holy Spirit. I was struggling with my inability to lead what I perceived to be a consistently fruitful life Monday through Saturday. I was excited about preaching on Sundays, but the rest of the week, the excitement about being a Christian seemed to leave me. I couldn't blame anybody or anything. Something just wasn't right inside me.

Annie had been to visit her mother, and while there, she bought a book titled *They Found the Secret* by Dr. V. Raymond Edmond. On a Saturday night, I found the book on a table by the door of my study. I picked it up and read the chapter about Hudson Taylor. He spoke about the passage in John 15:5 where Jesus says, "I am the vine, you are the branches." He asked, "How does the branch bear fruit? Not by struggle, but by resting in the vine."

I thought to myself, *That's where I am! I'm struggling when I should be resting.* It was as if my eyes were opened! I didn't have to struggle to be a Christian. I simply needed to rest in Him and allow Him to do the work in me. At that overwhelming realization, I immediately got on my face on the concrete floor of my study and cried and prayed to God. Before I got up, I knew that God had driven a second stake deep into my soul—that it wasn't me, but it was Jesus living inside me, who was going to do His work on this earth.

That was a totally new concept to me. I had never heard it preached. I had never heard it taught in seminary. I had never come across it in my studies prior to that night. Not me, but Christ inside me. The Holy Spirit had been the giver of power to me, but now He was resident in me to work through me. That truth changed my whole perspective on life and my entire relationship with God. No longer was my faith a matter of Jesus and me, but Jesus in me and working through me.

I assumed that the restlessness I had been feeling was the Lord bringing me to that new area of growth in my relationship with Him.

About that same time, we were facing a major challenge in the church—the opportunity to start a Christian school. I was afraid to do it, primarily because I didn't know anything about how to start a school, organize one, convince the

The Holy Spirit had been the giver of power to me, but now He was resident in me to work through me.

church we needed one, or fund one. For about six months, we prayed about it. Annie and I went back up to Fruitland to pray and rest for a couple of weeks at our house there.

When we returned to Miami, I was praying on the floor in our sunroom one day about the matter. I was mostly telling the Lord about how inadequate I felt and all the reasons why we couldn't build a school, and I heard the Lord speak to me crystal clear in my heart, *Here's your choice. You can do what I tell you and find out what I'll do with you, or you can spend the rest of your life wondering what I would have done if you had obeyed Me.*

I said, "God, sink or swim—I'm going!" I thought, *I'm not going to live the rest of my life wondering what would have happened if I had trusted God.* It was a trust issue for me. And we started the school. We called it the George Mueller Christian School, in honor of a man who never asked anybody for anything in funding his orphanage but who lived totally by faith and received everything he and the orphanage needed. Again, I assumed that the restlessness in my spirit had been the Lord leading me to that decision and to the building of the school.

Then one Sunday a pulpit committee from Bartow, Florida, visited the church in Miami. Now, every Sunday that I can remember our being in Miami, somebody from the church had invited us out to lunch. That particular Sunday, nobody did. We started to leave the church and found those eight men waiting for us, ready to take us to lunch. We went with them.

Over lunch, they began to ask me some questions that I felt were fairly irrelevant, so I finally said to them, "Listen, if you are interested in finding yourselves a pastor, here are the questions you need to ask him." I proceeded to give them a list. In retrospect, I no doubt was selling myself to them in the process, but that wasn't my intent at the time. I had no interest in going to their church. I didn't even know where Bartow was! I just wanted to help them out.

They told me that they had first visited the church in Miami a year before. One of the men said, "When you gave the invitation and then got down on your knees beside someone who walked forward, we knew we couldn't handle that in our church." He went on to say, "We've been to fifty-one churches since then, and God hasn't let us call any of the preachers we've heard. We know you're what we need."

I said, "No, you don't want me."

They said, "Yes, you're what we need."

I said, "I don't want to leave Miami. We love it here."

They said, "Pray about it."

So we did. And God made it very clear that He wanted us to move to Bartow, which we quickly learned was located between Lakeland and Orlando. The inner frustration and restlessness I had experienced for nearly a year vanished with that decision.

No sooner had we arrived in Bartow than God began dealing with me in yet a different way. Every time I'd get an idea for a sermon series, I'd find myself saying, "I'll put that off for a few months," and God would say, *No, preach it right now.* There was an urgency about our stay in Bartow that I had never experienced before.

I had been in Bartow only eleven months when I went to Alexandria, Virginia, to preach a week-long revival for a friend of mine. Every night after the service when I came back to my room, I felt very churned up on the inside. I kept saying, "God, what's going on? Please show me!"

On Wednesday night of that week, I pulled out a legal pad and drew a circle with five lines coming from it. I labeled each line as I considered that God must be about ready to

◆ do something in my life.

◆ change me.

◆ move me.

◆ do something new in my ministry.

◆ ?

I wrote a big question mark at the end of the fifth line to indicate that perhaps God was going to do something I had never thought about.

The next night as I got down on my knees and started to pray, I knew within me that God was saying, *I'm going to move you.*

I asked, "When?" Before my eyes, it seemed as if a screen appeared—the kind you project slides onto—and on that screen appeared a word. The word went diagonally from the lower left-hand corner to the upper right-hand corner, filling the screen with big bold black letters . . . SEPTEMBER.

I thought to myself, *It's April. That must be next September. I've been in Bartow only eleven months.* The following night when I got down to talk more to God, it was as if God had disappeared. I came home from the revival in Alexandria and told Annie what had happened.

The next Monday morning, I was sitting at my desk in my study when the phone rang, and it was my friend Felix Snipes. I hadn't heard from him in several years. He said, "How are you doing?" I said, "Fine, Felix. How are you?"

He said, "I want to talk to you about something you've never thought about." My mind immediately went back to that big question mark I had put on my legal pad in the hotel room in Alexandria.

Felix said, "People have been asking me who I would recommend as an associate pastor for our church, and you're the only person I can think of."

I said, "Why, Felix, you could probably think of fifty people."

He said, "But yours is the only name that keeps coming to my mind."

He went on to describe the situation at his church, and I said, "Felix, I wouldn't be interested in that at all. In the first place, you're asking me to be an associate pastor, and I'm not interested in being an associate pastor. Furthermore, I wouldn't be at all comfortable being an associate to a liberal pastor. And besides all that, I love it here in Bartow."

He said, "Would you pray about it?"

I said, "Sure, I'll pray about it." I hung up the phone and burst into tears. I thought, *What in the world is God doing?*

A couple of weeks later, a pulpit committee showed up at the church in Bartow. I told them, "No, I'm not interested."

Every week for the next several weeks, somebody from the church called me, and each time I said, "I'm not interested." Finally, one of the members of the pulpit committee called and said, "Can we come down for another visit?"

I said, "Well, I hate to see you waste your time, but it's okay with me if you come."

On that visit, eleven people came, including the senior

pastor. I met with them, and the senior pastor sat at the head of the table. The group gave its presentation, and then the senior pastor said, "Well, what's your answer?"

I said, "I can't give you an answer. God is going to have to tell me."

He said, "Well, what is God going to have to say to you?"

I said, "He's going to have to make it so crystal clear that I won't be able to stay here one more day."

The main thing I was wrestling with was the word SEP-TEMBER that I had seen so plainly in a vision in Alexandria. September was drawing ever closer, and I had heard from no other church except this one that kept calling me from Atlanta.

At that time, I had never even been to Atlanta, only through it on the old Highway 29 that went by Stone Mountain. As I was praying one day, it was as if I saw the skyline of Atlanta with a dark cloud hanging over it. I said to Annie, "If we go there, it's going to be a rough time."

As much as I didn't want to go to Atlanta, I couldn't quit praying about Atlanta, and finally I said to God, "God, if You really want me to go to Atlanta, I'll go, but I don't like it and I don't want to go." I grumbled all the way to Atlanta. And yet as much as I didn't want to go, the day I said I would go, the inner churning in my spirit ceased.

TAKING A STANCE OF OBEDIENCE

In looking back over the various places the Lord has led us to minister—Fruitland, Fairborne, Miami, Bartow, Atlanta —I can see a real progression. Each place was a preparation for what I was to encounter in the next place. Each place enabled me to learn certain lessons about how God works and about who God is.

What drove me wasn't a desire to succeed but a desire to be obedient to God. I knew that He was going to do something in my life, and that He was going to do something special with my life. So I was trusting Him.

If you experience a deep restlessness in your spirit—and you know that you are right with God—you, too, can trust God to be at work leading you into His next lesson, His next place of service, His next opportunity for you. He doesn't ask that you make those next moves happen. He asks only that you be obedient to His leading. You can trust Him to bring the right people and circumstances to pass.

In many ways, living within God's will is like riding a raft on a stream. There are rocks to avoid. There are times when you must put your oar in the water to help guide the raft into the current or away from danger. There are places to stop along the journey. But overall, there is no striving in floating downstream. The stream is one of God's creation; it flows according to God's principles. You must simply be willing to put yourself in God's raft and trust Him to give you the strength and wisdom to make a successful journey in the way that He has ordained for you to travel.

A woman came up to me one Sunday after the church

service and said, "Do you believe that a person can live by faith and still set goals?"

I said, "I don't know. I'll need to think about that a bit."

I went home that afternoon and spent several hours in my Bible seeking an answer to her question. I came away with the conclusion that, yes, a person can live by faith and still set goals—but here's the crux of the issue: *The goals must be God's goals for your life.*

There will no doubt be times when God says to you, *This is what I want you to do, and here are the steps you must take to get there.* That call from God becomes a goal. It is what you are seeking to do or accomplish for the Lord.

There are many other areas in God's Word where the Lord prescribes for us the general way in which we are to live. We are to live in certain ways—and learning to live the way Jesus lived takes discipline. We may need to set personal goals for acquiring more discipline in our lives.

In other areas of our lives, we need to unlearn something we've learned and to develop a new way of thinking. We may need to study something in particular or seek out God's principles for a certain area of our lives. Our topic of study may be a goal to us.

In still other areas of our lives, we may need to develop new habits to replace old ones that aren't in line with God's Word. Again, that takes discipline. We sometimes have to work diligently at retraining ourselves so that our automatic response in situations is the godly response.

All of these changes in the way we exercise our wills can be stated in terms of goals.

I am not at all opposed to setting goals, but I do believe it's beneficial for us to question ourselves continually about whether the goals we are setting are our self-manufactured goals or whether they are truly goals that the Lord has for us.

Here are several questions that I ask myself as I set goals:

◆ "Will it get me where I want to go—which is to a deeper and more intimate relationship with God, or to the accomplishment of something God has told me to do?"

◆ "Will it help make somebody else successful?"

◆ "Do I have to violate a spiritual principle to get there?"

◆ "Will it fulfill God's purpose for my life?"

FEELING INADEQUATE IN THE FACE OF GOD'S CALL

From time to time I meet people who say to me, "I think I heard God asking me to do something, but I'm having difficulty with what He has called me to do. I feel totally inadequate for the task." I consider this good news, not bad!

If you are in a position where you know that you *cannot* do something in and of your own strength, and that unless you completely trust God to do the work *in* you and *through* you, you will fail, then you are in the best possible position for the task to be accomplished! These are exciting days. These are days in which God will stretch you, grow you, and transform you into a person of even greater faith.

God knew before He asked you to do something that

you couldn't do it by yourself. His desire is that you will turn to Him and say, "I cannot do this, God. You can. I'm willing to be used and I'm willing to do whatever You tell me to do, but You'll have to provide all of the energy, the ideas, the resources, and the talent in order for this to get done." The person who truly says that with a humble heart before God is going to be the person God uses mightily to accomplish His purposes!

The Lord often shows us a general picture of what we are to do—and that broad overview tends to intimidate us and scare us. We need to realize that the Lord doesn't leave us with a giant goal or a great plan—He provides direction for all of the small steps that are necessary for getting to the big goal.

Ask the Lord to show you the first step that you need toward the goal. Recognize that it will be only a step. Be patient with yourself and with God's working in you. Do what He shows you to do with all your strength, might, and talent. And then look for the second step that He leads you to take.

The Lord doesn't catapult us into greatness; He grows us into spiritual maturity.

He stretches us slowly so that we don't break.

He expands our vision slowly so that we can take in all of the details of what He desires to accomplish.

He causes us to grow slowly so that we stay balanced.

The unfolding of God's plan for our lives is a process. Expect to be engaged in that process for the rest of your life.

Beware of coming to the point where you say, "That's

enough. I'm comfortable with this. I'm satisfied with what has been done. I've arrived."

God is never committed to leaving us on a plateau. His desire is that we continue to grow ever more into the likeness of His Son, Jesus Christ. That's a lifelong journey! None of us will ever fully arrive at that point, but we are always to be walking toward it.

He'll do whatever it takes to prod us toward His higher places. He'll make us restless with where we are. He'll make us hunger and thirst for more of Him. He'll cause us to desire things we never dreamed of desiring in our relationship with Him.

Although we are to develop good relationships and build meaningful projects wherever we are, we are also to be in a state of willingness to move on if that is what God desires for us. We can trust, once again, that God will lead us elsewhere only for our benefit and for the benefit of others.

Throughout the Scriptures, we see where the Lord calls us sojourners, travelers, wanderers. Heaven is our ultimate home, and until we arrive there, everything else is a journey to get there. We are never to sit down and take our ease and be satisfied that we have enough of God, that we know God with sufficient intimacy, or that God is finished with us.

We are continually to be in His making. His process of transforming us, and of re-creating us, continues every day of our lives.

Being willing to grow is a challenge for many people. Most of us are creatures of habit. We resist change. Sometimes we get angry that God overturns our apple carts or upsets our carefully crafted plans.

If you are angry with God for the changes He's leading you to make or for the new paths He's showing you to walk, you can express that anger to God. He's big enough to take it. It will be part of your being honest before the Lord about how you feel.

You can say to the Lord, "I don't understand this. I don't like this. I'm not happy about this. I'm upset." Your anger won't change the way God feels about you. It also won't change His plans. You may feel better if you vent your feelings. And, eventually, you'll admit, "Yes, that was the best thing." One day you'll look back and say, "I'm so glad God directed me in that way."

Consider how a mother and father relate to their child. The child may not want to do what the parent says to do—in fact, most children don't want to do whatever their parents tell them to do. They might complain steadily. And yet the parent doesn't love the child any less. And if the parent is wise, the parent won't give in on a matter in which the parent knows the decision is best for the child.

We may not feel like doing God's will, but again, we don't walk by feelings in following the Lord. We walk by faith in what God says is best for us. It's all right—and even good and healthy—for us to vent our feelings. It's not all right to sin or willfully walk away from God's plan. In the end, we must do what God calls us to do, and change in the ways God asks us to change, if we are truly going to experience God's best—which will be what we come to know as the most joyful, fulfilling, purposeful way to live.

LOOK FOR MULTIPLE JOY IN OBEYING GOD'S WILL

Obeying God's will in your life will eventually include some form of giving. Sometimes that giving may hurt.

We were receiving money one Sunday in 1980 toward our new church property, and people were coming forward to give all kinds of things—cars, houses, property. A woman walked forward and took off a large gold bracelet and put it in my hand. She said to me, "This is the most valuable thing I own." (The bracelet was, indeed, valuable. It sold for $17,000 when we turned it in for the church building fund.)

Up to that moment, I thought our family had given everything we could possibly give—we had sold a car and our travel trailer and given the money to the building fund. When the woman dropped that gold bracelet into my hand, however, the Lord spoke in my heart and said, *You've never given Me anything but money.*

My thoughts turned immediately to my cameras. Now, I love to take photographs. That's my hobby. I'd rather be off on a trip taking photographs than doing just about anything else but preaching and being with God's people. Down through the years, I had acquired quite a bit of camera gear. And I thought, *Oh, no, Lord, that's asking too much.* But I knew instantly that selling my cameras was what I had to do.

The next day, I got all my camera equipment together and took it down to a friend who bought and sold used camera equipment. I said to him, "I'm here to sell my equipment."

He said, "Why are you doing that?"

I said, "Well, we are buying this property for the church, and the Lord has laid a certain amount on my heart to give. I've sold a car and my travel trailer and given that money, but I still need to give more. What can you give me for my cameras? I know you'll treat me right."

I had felt strongly impressed that we were to give at least $5,000 more than we had given. I had saved about $1,600. The camera store owner went into the back and figured up what he could give me on my cameras, and he came back and said, "How does $3,420 sound?" I said, "That's perfect."

I gave the $5,000 the next service. For about two or three weeks afterward, however, I was feeling some sense of loss. I had given my cameras, but emotionally, I was still holding on to them. The day came when the Lord reminded me of the verse in the Bible that says, "Where your treasure is, there your heart will be also" (Matt. 6:21). I had to ask myself, "Is my heart tied up in my cameras, or is my heart tied up in what the Lord is doing?" And I decided that I would choose, by my will, to link my heart to what God was doing in our midst rather than to a collection of shutters and lenses and film holders.

In that moment, I truly gave those cameras to the Lord. I turned them over to Him in my heart, and I became a cheerful giver before the Lord.

Several months later, a woman rang the doorbell of my house. When I answered the door, she said, "Are you Charles Stanley?"

I said, "Yes, ma'am."

She said, "Here!" and she handed me a suitcase and a paper bag. Then she walked away. I started to ask her, "What is this? Why are you giving me this?" but she left before I could get the questions out of my mouth.

I brought the suitcase and paper bag inside, and I found in them every single item of the camera gear that I had sold and given to the Lord. Every camera body, every lens, and every filter was there.

I went down to the store, and the owner looked at me and said, "Don't ask me." He had promised never to reveal the identity of the person who bought my equipment and gave it back to me.

I've had a *triple* joy from that experience of giving my cameras. The single joy was the genuine joy of giving those cameras to the Lord—of truly giving them out of my heart as sacrificial giving of treasure to the house of God. That joy would have stayed with me all my life, even if I had never seen those cameras again. But that isn't the way God works. His Word says, "Give, and it will be given to you: good measure, pressed down, shaken together, and running over will be put into your bosom" (Luke 6:38). The Lord could have chosen to give me back anything He wanted. He had no obligation to give me back those cameras. And yet, that was His pleasure, and I had the double joy of receiving back my camera gear.

The triple joy has come in recent years as the Lord has allowed me to publish several books that include photos I've taken.

I couldn't help being reminded of Simon Peter lending his fishing boat to Jesus. He, too, experienced a multiple joy. Peter had the joy of giving his boat to Jesus so that Jesus could use it as an offshore pulpit and teach the multitudes from it. Then Jesus gave the boat back to Peter but with the command, "Launch out into the deep and let down your nets for a catch" (Luke 5:4). After protesting, Peter did what Jesus said, and he and his partners caught such a load of fish that their nets began to break and their boats nearly capsized.

Out of that experience, Jesus called Peter to come and follow Him. He said to Peter, "From now on you will catch men" (Luke 5:10).

We don't know how Peter felt about giving his boat to Jesus, but we do know that Peter certainly didn't feel like launching out into the deep for that catch of fish. He had said grudgingly, "Master, we have toiled all night and caught nothing; nevertheless at Your word I will let down the net" (Luke 5:5). We also know that Peter's response to the miracle catch of fish was one of astonishment and fear. Peter fell at Jesus' knees, saying, "Depart from me, for I am a sinful man, O Lord!" (Luke 5:8).

The point is, however, that Peter obeyed Jesus in both cases. He launched his boat. He followed Jesus. And in so doing, the Lord led him into an entirely new path—one that was to last Peter's entire lifetime.

Ultimately, we must do as Peter did. We are called to obey, no matter how much God's plan signals a change in our lives. We are called to give. When we do, the Lord multiplies our joy and gives us a sense of fulfillment.

MAKING HIS PLAN YOUR PLAN

Early in my ministry, I came across a statement from Oswald Chambers that said, in effect, "Make your ultimate goal your own personal relationship with Him." I know that if my relationship with God is right, I'm going to be able to hear Him and know His direction. If I get off track, He's going to pull me onto the track.

Now, the Lord may allow me to get off track and suffer and get hurt, and get blasted and shattered for my own good, but He isn't going to let me get away from His will for my life if I'm truly seeking to be in right relationship with Him. The conviction of the Holy Spirit is always going to be there, tugging me and pulling at me to get back onto the track He's established for my life.

I firmly believe that if God is in control of my life, He's going to show me what to do. I can make my plans, but I'd better be open to His changing my plans. Ultimately, I want my plan to be His plan.

One way that God speaks to me is through repetition. An idea will come to me as a very strong impression. That impression will come again and again until it becomes a concern. The concern will not leave but will grow into a conviction. The conviction becomes deeper and deeper until I can no longer escape it or forget it. With the conviction comes a sureness that I am willing to stake my life on.

I never ask others to give me authority to do something that I'm not willing to stake my life on. I've got to be that certain that I'm in the will of God before I'll ask for authority to take actions that involve other people.

A number of years ago, I asked the church to give me the authority to buy all the property we needed without telling them where it was or how much it was going to cost. They granted me that authority.

For my part, I knew that I wasn't going to pursue the purchase of a piece of property unless God directed me to it, made it a conviction of my heart, and provided the money. As He began to lead, I purchased on behalf of the church. What was the result? Over the years, we purchased property around the church in downtown Atlanta and the gain more than tripled the amount spent.

Very often the Lord doesn't show us the full plan or all the details. We simply do what He tells us to do next. We ask Him to lead us, and we do the thing that He shows us to do immediately. Having done that next thing, we trust Him for guidance and then take the next step He reveals.

CONFIRMING GOD'S WILL

Along the way, we must continually be looking for confirmation that what we are doing truly is God's will. In some ways, it is like taking a trip along a route we've never traveled before. We continually look for highway signs confirming that we are on the right road.

Again, I believe it's especially important to get confirmation for something that you believe is God's will in matters where other people are involved. If God reveals something to you as the right move to make, He'll also reveal it to others who are involved. And how do you check that?

◆ Find an incident in God's Word that confirms to you that you are acting in God's will. If what you believe God is telling you is contrary to God's Word, you are misreading God's will. God's will for you today will always line up with

His eternal Word. Make certain that what you find in God's Word is a principle of God, not just an example in someone's life. If it's a principle of God, it will appear in more than one place in God's Word.

◆ Seek out the advice of wise and trustworthy counselors. Go to people of prayer who are accustomed to hearing God's voice, who know God's Word, and who have your best interests at heart. Find people who will speak the truth to you, not just tell you what they think you want to hear.

At times, God may send a wise counselor to you that you aren't expecting. Just a few months ago, someone came up to me after a board meeting and brought up a matter that had not been discussed in the meeting. He said, "You have got to do something on this."

I had been sensing in my heart for some time that I needed to take action in the matter he mentioned, but I had not been sure about what I should do or when I should act. His words to me, "You need to do something now," were wise counsel. I took his words—which came to me unexpectedly and on his initiative, not mine—as a signal from God that He was shoving me toward action.

Don't overlook the presence of wise counselors that God may have already placed in your midst. Many times I see corporate leaders looking to outside consultants to help them solve their internal problems; I can't help wondering if their own people might not have been able to give them the most accurate, best advice.

If we are facing a major decision at the church or in the In Touch radio and television ministry, I always put it on the table before the whole staff. Everybody present knows that it's okay to say anything and everything relevant to the issue. All the while the matter is being discussed, I sit back and listen. It's as if the Holy Spirit is sifting that information before me. I also listen deep within to what the Lord is saying inside me. If something is God's will for us as a ministry, there's nearly always consensus that an action is right to take, and there's agreement about timing. If something is not God's will, one or more of us will have a strong check in our spirits. We'll sense that God is saying, *No,* or *Not now,* or *Do this instead.*

Ultimately, I'm the one who is responsible for the final decision, and I'm the one who has to live with the decisions I make.

TAKING OWNERSHIP FOR YOUR DECISIONS

That's true for every person. You are the one who is going to have to live with the decisions you make. You are the one who is going to have to say, "Yes, God is in this move," or "No, God is saying something else." Nobody else is responsible for the moves you make in God's will—not your pastor, your spiritual advisor, your spouse, your family, or your children. That's why it's so vital that you learn to hear God's voice for yourself, and that you learn how to confirm what He says to you.

A few years ago, we had found a piece of property that seemed to be right for the needs we were facing at that time in our In Touch ministry. The price of the property was $2,750,000—a sizable amount. All signals seemed to be go,

and some of our executive staff were in agreement that the
piece of property seemed right for us.

Every time I prayed about buying that property, however, I felt God speaking in my spirit, *Don't do that.* I told the
staff, "We aren't going to buy that property." They asked me
why, and I told them God was saying no. I suggested that we
go away and pray for a couple of days about the purchase. I
knew that if the Lord truly was speaking to me, He would
also speak to the others involved in making the decision. He
would show them that the purchase of the building wasn't
His plan. As we prayed for those two days, He did reveal that
to them. The final outcome was that God led us to an even
better piece of property, and He sovereignly provided the
money with which to buy it through a gift!

It's easy to give in to a group that is in strong favor of
something. It's very difficult to stand up and be the only
negative vote. On another occasion, my staff was very eager to
take a particular action, and although I didn't think it would
work, I decided to go along with the decision. The matter
turned out to be a disaster. I should have said no.

On other occasions, I've had an idea, and when I sub-
jected it to the group process, I've come to realize that I was
the one who was about to make a mistake. I've had to admit
to myself and to them, "That was the wrong way to go. The
way you've suggested is right."

The Lord's will is always going to be a win-win proposi-
tion for everybody involved. The devil is the only one who is
ever going to lose when it comes to matters of God's will.
Because God's will is of benefit to all His children, He reveals
and confirms His will liberally. He doesn't just tell one per-

son in one place at one time what He desires to see accomplished. He may start by telling just one person, but ultimately, He'll confirm that truth to anybody who is open to hearing it.

Now, once in a while, I know that as a leader I need to take a bold first step. Others may not yet have caught the vision, or they may not yet have heard God. In those moments—when I know I am bucking the tide of my close associates—I nearly always have an overwhelming feeling inside me that I cannot escape. I know that I must take action or I will be in disobedience to God. At the same time, I have a strong sense of being very vulnerable. I know that I am the only one who is shouldering the responsibility for that action. I must be willing to stand before God and say, "I take sole responsibility for this."

DISCOVERING GOD'S TIMING

Just as the Lord has a right thing for you to do, a right path in which you are to walk, and a right growth pattern for your faith, so, too, He has a right timing for each step He leads you to take.

A restlessness in spirit often manifests itself as a tendency to run past God's will. You may know what God wants you to do, and in eagerness to get the job done, you forget that God also has a perfect timetable for accomplishing His will.

As you receive confirmation that God wants you to take a specific action or make a specific move, ask Him to reveal to you when He wants you to act or move. Numerous times in the Scriptures we find advantage in waiting on the Lord. Waiting means, in part, saying to the Lord, "Is now the time? I'm waiting until You give me the green light before I go."

As you read through these verses from some psalms, notice the great benefits of waiting for God's perfect timing:

> Let integrity and uprightness preserve me,
> For I wait for You (Ps. 25:21).

> Wait on the LORD;
> Be of good courage,
> And He shall strengthen your heart;
> Wait, I say, on the LORD! (Ps. 27:14).

> Wait on the LORD,
> And keep His way,
> And He shall exalt you to inherit the land;
> When the wicked are cut off,
>   you shall see it (Ps. 37:34).

> I will wait for You,
> O You his Strength;
> For God is my defense (Ps. 59:9).

If you have a pattern of getting ahead of God's timing, ask yourself, "What am I looking for in life? Why do I keep running right past God's will in trying to get it? What am I in a hurry for?"

If you have a pattern in your life of getting ahead of God's timing, ask yourself, "What am I looking for in life? Why do I keep running right past God's will in trying to get it? What am I in a hurry for?"

Do you feel that time will run out before you get your

mission accomplished? God has all of time and eternity under His control. He won't direct you to do a job you don't have time to finish.

Are you in a hurry to get more power, fame, or money —to establish your reputation and your own kingdom on this earth? God's kingdom is the only one that really counts. He isn't interested in helping you build your personal little kingdom.

Are you champing at the bit to try out a new skill or to test a new ability? God's processes have an order and a rhythm to them. Don't overextend where you are in God's growth pattern.

The disadvantages of getting ahead of God are also evident throughout the Bible. Abraham and Sarah got ahead of God's plan in Abraham's fathering of a child through Hagar. Peter was notorious for trying to get ahead of God's plan, even to the slicing off of a man's ear in the Garden of Gethsemane.

Jesus, on the other hand, never showed up too early or too late. He always arrived right on time in keeping with what the Father was doing.

One of my favorite passages of Scripture is Psalm 62:1–2:

> Truly my soul silently waits for God;
> From Him comes my salvation.
> He only is my rock and my salvation;
> He is my defense;
> I shall not be greatly moved.

Learning to wait on God's timing is one of the hallmarks of the mature Christian life.

How can you know when God is saying *Move, now!* or *Now's the time?*

When you say to the Lord, "I'm trusting You to show me when to move," it is then the Lord's responsibility to show you when to take action. He'll plant an urgency in your heart that the time is at hand. He may awaken you in the middle of the night with a deep impression that you are to take action the next day, or He may put such a conviction in your heart about a certain date or time that you won't be able to escape it. If you are diligently seeking and anticipating and expecting God to give you a go signal, He will—and you will know it when you experience it.

Some people are eager to throw out fleeces as Gideon did in order to determine the surety of God's will to them. They say, "If this happens, I'll do that, but if that happens, I'll do this." It's as if they are giving God a true-false or multiple-choice test. Even though this matter of putting out a fleece is in the Bible, I don't believe God intended it as a principle for all to follow, and, therefore, I don't recommend that people devise tests for God. In part, people can figure out how to manipulate things so that the answer they get is the answer they want. Other people who may know about the fleece can also alter the results. A more reliable, consistent approach to determining God's will, in my opinion, is simply to ask Him, "Lord, what is it that You want me to do?"

That leaves the door open for God to tell us whatever He desires. He isn't limited to the choices that we put before Him.

REACHING A STATE OF TRUE
CONTENTMENT

The opposite of a continual feeling of restlessness and frustration is contentment. Contentment is the shalom peace of the Bible—a place of wholeness and assurance.

That type of peace doesn't depend on outer circumstances.

The world is always going to have irritants in it. Unwise decisions and sinful situations abound. They have nothing, however, to do with the state of your inner soul. You can be content on the inside, no matter what kinds and amounts of sin or error swirl around you.

The apostle Paul was sitting in a Roman prison, facing all kinds of persecution and ridicule from others, when he wrote, "I have learned in whatever state I am, to be content: I know how to be abased, and I know how to abound. Everywhere and in all things I have learned both to be full and to be hungry, both to abound and to suffer need" (Phil. 4:11–12).

How did Paul find this inner contentment?

By focusing on the sovereignty of God rather than on the will of people.

By praising and thanking God rather than criticizing others.

By putting trust in God to deal with the future rather than continually looking at the past.

By trusting in God to make all things right rather than distrusting human ability.

Paul concluded his statement about inner contentment

by saying, "I can do all things through Christ who strengthens me" (Phil. 4:13). As Paul turned his attention to Christ and away from his circumstances and detractors, he received strength.

His contentment didn't rest in just denying the outside world or the facts related to his situation. His contentment flowed from his trust in Christ.

Whether your inner restlessness comes from unresolved issues in your past or it is a God-given frustration intended to draw you deeper into the Lord's will, the answer to restlessness comes as you trust God.

You trust Him to be your shelter, your safety from life's storms and turmoil.

You trust Him to be your shield against the assaults of the enemy that try to catch you off guard, pull you off track, or cause you to stumble.

You trust Him to be your wisdom against error and false starts.

You trust Him to be your peace.

Claim the words of Jesus as your own: "Peace I leave with you, My peace I give to you; not as the world gives do I give to you. Let not your heart be troubled, neither let it be afraid" (John 14:27). The peace that Jesus gives is the "peace of God, which surpasses all understanding"—a peace that "will guard your hearts and minds"(Phil. 4:7).

Are you frustrated and restless today? Above all else, say to the Lord, "I need for You to settle me and to give me Your peace."

Then look for Him to fill your heart with His presence.

TRUTH CAPSULE

When you are feeling restless or frustrated . . .

1. Examine your heart. Are you running from something that you need to face? If so, ask the Lord to reveal to you the reason for frustration and to give you the courage to face it head-on.

2. Look for God to bring about a change in your life. Trust Him to lead you into His path for you. As you begin to sense God's direction, confirm His word to you. Ask the Lord to reveal not only what He desires for you to do but when He desires for you to take action.

3. Ask the Lord to give you His peace.

My excess baggage from frustration.

_____

_____

_____

_____

_____

_____

_____

_____

_____

How I can lighten this load.

_____

_____

_____

_____

_____

_____

_____

_____

God is the source of my strength.

Words
of
comfort
and
healing
to
those
who
are

7

BURNED OUT

*D*uring those years of striving for perfection and seeking approval in my ministry, I knew what I was doing—at least to an extent. I knew at some level of understanding that I was working too hard for an impossible ideal and expecting too much of myself and others. How did I justify my behavior?

> *I* rationalized my behavior by saying, "God made me this way." Much of what I thought I was doing for God, I was really doing for Charles Stanley. ◆

Well, I handled it like a perfectionist who was continually seeking approval! I blamed my behavior on everybody else and refused to be critical of myself. I rationalized my behavior by saying, "God made me this way."

The result was that I got on a downward spiral of more and more work in an effort to get better and better and to receive more and more approval. Eventually, I crashed hard.

In 1977, I was doing two thirty-minute television programs plus the Sunday morning television program that came from the church in addition to everything else I was doing as a pastor. I noticed that instead of just being tired on Monday —which is normal for a pastor after having preached Sunday morning and Sunday night—I was tired on Tuesday. Pretty soon I was tired on Wednesday, too. Then I realized that I was just as tired on Saturday as I was on Monday morning.

I went to the hospital three times that year and had all kinds of tests, and each time, the doctors found nothing wrong. I'd tell my physician, "There's nothing wrong. I'm just tired." I'd try to take a little break, but it was never a long enough break to really help me.

Stephen Olford came to my church one weekend to preach, and on Saturday night, my wife and I went with him and his wife to have dinner at a downtown hotel.

We went to the same hotel where we had gone three years before. At that time Dr. Olford had told us about the physical problems he had experienced. I remember thinking as he shared his story, *I'm never going to let that happen to me.*

Yet, there we were three years later, and he was asking me, "How are you doing?"

I said, "Fine."

My wife said, "No, you're not. Tell him the truth."

So I told him about my exhaustion, and he said, "You're going to the hospital tonight."

I said, "No, I'm not. You're preaching for our Missions Sunday service in the morning, and I've got to be there."

He said, "No, you don't. And furthermore, I'm going to arrange for twelve of the best preachers in the nation to come and preach for you every Sunday for the next three months."

I said, "Oh, I don't know about all that."

Dr. Olford did just what he said, however. He and his wife and Annie drove me to the hospital and checked me in. The next morning after he had preached, he called a meeting of the deacons of the church and said to them, "If you want this man alive, you've got to give him a leave of three months, six months, whatever it takes."

He and one of the deacons came to see me in the hospital that same Sunday night, and they said, "We forbid you to come back to preach at the church for at least three months." Dr. Olford then arranged for outstanding preachers to fill the pulpit the next twelve Sundays, a different person each week.

I went from the hospital in Atlanta to a medical center in Virginia for two weeks to have a thorough series of tests. Every morning I had tests, and in the afternoons, I'd walk and pray. The doctors didn't find anything physically wrong —no heart problems, no ulcers. I was just worn out.

A man in our church arranged for me to go to a small island about two and a quarter miles long and a quarter of a mile wide at its widest point. The island is located about two hundred miles directly east of West Palm Beach. Only 230 people live on it, and they had no hotels, no automobiles, and only two telephones at the time. Annie couldn't go with me since we were in the process of building a house. So Andy, my son, took a few months leave from his schooling, and he and I went to the island for five weeks. We fished, walked, swam, read, studied, and prayed.

It sounds idyllic.

When you've been running as fast as you can, however, and you are feeling driven twenty-four hours a day, getting off to an isolated place like that is a shock. Suddenly, there's nothing to drive toward! There's nobody around to applaud you. There's nothing to get up for or to keep you going. It was like hitting a wall.

I also felt so drained that I wondered if I'd ever regain sufficient strength to function normally. I had lots of self-doubt to go along with the exhaustion.

I had no difficulty talking to God, and I certainly didn't place any blame on Him for the situation I was in. I knew that the problem was resident in me. I was feeling driven to succeed. I was committed to so many things, and I didn't know where to get off the wheel that was spinning. I wanted to stop wearing myself out—but I didn't know how to stop doing all that I was doing. I had a sense that I needed to stop overextending myself, but at the same time, I didn't know which activity to drop.

Ultimately, I didn't want to give anything up. I wanted to do everything I was doing. I wanted to achieve everything I was achieving. I'd look at a situation and say to myself, "Well, this is working—so why give that up?" And so it went for everything I was doing.

I don't know why I felt I had to do so much. Perhaps I was trying to prove to myself that I could do everything in which I was involved. Perhaps I was responding to the approval I was receiving. Perhaps it was related to the circumstances facing me in the church at that time.

I had a strong desire to see souls saved and to see the pews of the church filled with people. I had an equally strong desire to make sure that all of the programs at the church functioned to serve the people. I had big goals in lots of areas. I kept my goals continually in front of me. Short range. Middle range. Long range. I had them all lined up, and I was committed to making them happen, do or die. I had a strong desire to reach those goals as quickly as possible, but I had too little help. When you have that combination, the tendency is to spread yourself very thin and to become overextended. I had done just that.

The number one person who was driving me was me!

Now, if you had asked me at the time whether I was driven, I would have said to you, "No. I just love God." In looking back, I realize that much of what I thought I was doing for God, I was really doing for Charles Stanley. Much of my prayer life was focused on what I wanted to achieve— what I wanted to accomplish for the church.

I had goals for my life, goals for the family, and seven major goals for the church. The goals were diverse—from personal finances to family health to church membership. I kept them in a big notebook and referred to them often. My relationship with God was based primarily on His helping me to get things done. I knew He had the power to do it, and I thought that if I just believed hard enough and trusted Him to act, the goals would be reached.

I don't think I've ever felt I could do anything significant on my own. I frequently told God how inadequate I felt and how I couldn't do anything if He didn't do it. Looking back now, I realize that I was deceived about my motivations. In many ways, the motivations were masked by the success. Things were working! The church was growing! Goals were being met. I didn't want to stop. In point of fact, all seven of the goals I had set for the church to reach by 1990 were reached long before that.

I never asked God for permission to stop any of the

activities in which I was involved. I asked Him only for strength to do more.

There's a big difference between enjoying the accomplishment of a goal and enjoying the process of working toward that goal. I enjoyed the results of what I was doing, but I didn't enjoy the activities themselves. For example, I liked the fact that we had a successful thirty-minute television program that came from the pastor's study. But I hated the emotional drain of those programs—doing them three or more at a time, having to concentrate completely on the camera with no audience present, needing to supply all of the emotional energy and strength to carry that type of format.

And in the process of wanting to do it all and have it all, I found myself utterly exhausted physically, mentally, and emotionally.

My island get-away helped me to recover a certain degree of physical and mental strength. At least part of my healing had begun by the time I returned to Atlanta. Upon my return, I said to the carpenter who was building our house, "Put me to work." I went over to the construction site every day and worked as a carpenter's helper. Working with my hands for a month was excellent therapy.

Finally, after twelve weeks, I returned to the church. I found attendance up, the offering up, and the people happy. God had taken good care of the flock!

It took nearly ten more months, however, for me to feel that I was fully back physically. I remember the moment when I stepped into the pulpit and said, "I feel good!"

In the course of that full experience and the process of recuperation, I learned several principles.

Principle #1: Mental and emotional burnout cannot be remedied unless you also deal with the physical burnout

Don't push yourself beyond the point of being tired. To do so is to suffer exhaustion—a complete depletion of your strength and energy. If you find yourself already at that point of exhaustion, take the time you need to rest and to refuel yourself. The first step toward being healed of burnout nearly always includes a period of prolonged rest coupled with good nutrition.

Principle #2: Physical burnout directly affects the mind and emotions

A woman came to me recently and said, "Pastor Stanley, I have no energy. I feel tired all the time."

I asked her, "What do you think about the most?"

She said, "All the things I have to do."

I said, "That's your real problem. You've got your mind wrapped around the wrong things."

I went on to ask her, "How much time do you spend reading the Word or praying?"

She said, "I hardly ever read the Bible or pray. I just don't have the time."

I said, "That's the problem. The busier you are in life, the more you *need* to have time to pray and to read God's

Word. You need to make His Word and your relationship with Him the number one priority in your life."

The woman was not an isolated case. I encounter many people who are stressed out and living on the edge. They are wearing out fast. Something inside them has sprung a leak, and their energy and joy are draining away.

If you are tired all the time, ask yourself,

◆ "What am I thinking about all the time?"
◆ "What troubles me the most?"
◆ "What am I worried about?"

The real issue is not the exhaustion and stress but the problem that is absorbing all of your attention and emotional energy. Face up to that issue first, and the likelihood is that your energy and joy will come back.

*F*ace up to what is absorbing all of your attention and emotional energy, and the likelihood is that your energy and joy will come back.

Principle #3: When feeling burned out, go back to the basics of your life in Christ

If you can honestly say that you're not troubled by something, the cause of your exhaustion may be a physical problem. See a physician. Honestly describe how you feel.

If there's no physical problem and you aren't troubled by anything in your emotions, ask yourself whether you have let your relationship with the Lord slide.

Have you let the weight of the world settle on your shoulders unaware rather than shift the weight of the world over to the Lord?

Are you disappointed that the world isn't providing you the happiness you seek rather than trusting the Lord to give you His joy?

Are you struggling with doubts and nagging fears about the purpose and meaning of your life rather than finding your fulfillment in the Lord?

It may well be time for you to take stock of your life and say, "I've got to return to basics." The basics for any Christian are threefold:

◆ *God's Word.* Spend time every day in God's Word. I don't prescribe a certain amount of reading or a certain amount of time. But do spend time every day reading your Bible. What you read becomes part of you. It becomes the way you think and respond to life. It becomes your very nature, your character, your attitude, your mind-set.

God's Word never causes us to feel exhausted, frustrated, anxious, or fretful. God's Word brings peace, hope, rest, and soundness of heart and mind.

◆ *Prayer.* Spend time every day talking to God. Tell Him how you feel. Thank Him for the good things you are experiencing in your life. Praise Him for the good things of the past. Ask Him for the things you need. Share with Him your worries, hopes, desires, fears, and concerns. Listen for Him to speak His words of comfort, counsel, and direction. Develop a walking-and-talking relationship with the Lord.

◆ *Fellowship with other believers.* Get involved in a church with others who believe about God's Word the way you believe. Attend regularly. Volunteer your services in an area where you can share your talents and gifts. Make friends of those with whom you worship.

If you are too busy to attend church, too tired to pray, or too preoccupied to read God's Word, take another look at your priorities. It's time to make a change and to put your relationship with God first. As Matthew 6:33 says, "Seek first the kingdom of God and His righteousness, and all these things shall be added to you"—including time, a spirit of relaxation, and the joy of living!

Principle #4: Make a decision to do only what the Lord requires

If you are too busy to attend church, too tired to pray, or too preoccupied to read God's Word, take another look at your priorities.

Maybe you can honestly say, "I am not troubled emotionally. I am physically healthy. I have a daily, intimate relationship with the Lord. And I'm still exhausted."

If that's the case, you may simply be trying to do too much in your life. You may very well be doing more than God expects you to do or wants you to do.

God will never call you to do something unless He also provides the means for you to have the energy and resources to accomplish His task. You may have to work hard, but God never requires that you have a nervous, emotional, or physical breakdown in the process. As successful and busy as Jesus was in His ministry, He frequently took time away from the crowds. He knew how to relax and renew His strength physically, emotionally, and spiritually. Let Him be your example.

God does not commit Himself to helping us do everything *we* want to do in our lives. He is committed to helping us do only things that *He* wants us to do. God spends His wisdom, His energy, and His knowledge and understanding not on the fringes of what we want to do in life but on what He wants to see accomplished.

The Lord lets us experience exhaustion and feelings of being burned out to teach us His lessons:

◆ That we are doing more than He is actually requiring us to do.

◆ That we have our priorities out of order.

◆ That we aren't putting Him first.

◆ That we are trying to do too many good things at the same time.

When I returned from my period of recuperation, I immediately dropped two of the television programs, and I limited myself to pastoring the church. I laid low and didn't allow myself to get caught up in too many things that weren't related to the church or my family. I completely changed my schedule. I no longer committed myself to a full week of activities. In place of those activities, I set aside unscheduled days for prayer and study.

If you are worn out today, I suggest that you do five things:

1. *Back off everything that you are doing and reappraise your life.* It may be helpful to get away for a day, a weekend, or a few days—even a week or two. Spend at least part of this time praying and fasting. Prayer will help you focus your attention on what God wants you to do. Fasting tends to clear away your preoccupation with things of this world and to help you see priorities and situations more clearly.

2. *Make a list of everything that you are doing and the time required for each activity.* Get a good understanding of just how you are spending your time. Many people are surprised to see where they are devoting most of their time or to discover how much time certain activities, chores, or hobbies take.

3. *Evaluate how much personal energy is required for each activity.* Sometimes you may not spend much time doing a task, but

*B*ack off everything that you are doing and reappraise your life.

the task may require a great deal of emotional or physical energy. As I mentioned earlier, one of the two half-hour television programs I was doing in 1977 was a program that was taped without an audience. I discovered that it took a great deal more emotional, mental, and spiritual energy for me to do that program than to do the one with an audience. Yet both programs took about the same amount of time to do. Guess which program was the first to go.

4. *Look for trends and patterns among the activities you have listed.* Ask yourself, "Do I have a balance between mental and physical activities? Have I included spiritual activities on my list? Do I take sufficient time for rest and play? Why am I doing the things that I am doing?"

Many people find that they are doing things because they think others expect them to do them. That may or may not be true. But even if it is true, our motivation for doing things should not be solely because others ask us, want us, or require us to do them.

You may say to yourself, "But if I don't do these things —if I don't accomplish this much—other people will think I'm a failure."

It doesn't make any difference what others think. It only matters what God thinks, and He'll never require you to do things that are beyond your physical, emotional, or mental ability. You can never truly please other people anyway. No matter what you do—or how much of it you do —there will always be somebody who is displeased. The expectations of people are fickle. They change frequently. What others expect of you today isn't likely to be what they expect of you next week or next year. What others

*Y*ou may say to yourself, "But if I don't do these things —if I don't accomplish this much—other people will think I'm a failure."

want you to do today, they may not even think about or remember next month!

Don't let the expectations, requests, or desires of others drive you. If you do, you'll never have peace in your heart.

5. *With your evaluation of activities, time, and energy before you, ask the Lord to reveal to you what is truly important to Him—and to show you where you need to spend more time, where you need to spend less time, and what activities you might drop.* Ask about each activity, "Lord, is this something You really want me to do—and something You want me to do right now? Do You really want me to spend this much time at it? Do You want me to spend more time?"

Don't be bound to your list. Also ask the Lord, "Is there something else You'd rather I spend my time doing? Is there something I'm not doing that You would like for me to do?"

Ask yourself, "What are the consequences of taking a new position? What are the consequences of making another choice? What are the consequences of taking the action I propose to take?"

Are you willing to live with the consequences? Are you willing to pay the price of persecution from those who may not understand what you are doing—and persecution from those who will never understand the will of God?

Be suspicious of doing things the way the majority of people do them. Note that I did not say the majority of Bible-believing Christians—rather, the majority of people at large. The crowd is nearly always wrong, at least to a degree. The crowd isn't interested in doing things God's way, following God's will, or taking a stand based on the Bible. If the masses are running in a particular direction, back off and look at the situation.

Be equally suspicious of prevailing public opinion or opinions that are widely held in our society.

Society says a number of things to us that don't line up with God's Word. A man said to me that his idea of success had once been to marry a beauty queen, live in a big house in a fine neighborhood, and drive a Cadillac. He said, "I've gained all those things, and I'm miserable." He had let society rather than the Word of God define success for him.

Principle #5: Let God take control, and give Him the responsibility

One of the most positive results of my recuperation was that I gave up feeling that I had to have control over every detail and every activity of the church.

The person who attempts to control everything is really saying in the heart, "God, I don't think You can control this situation." Such a person tends to jump in and help God or to help others help God. I have come to the place in my life where I know with certainty that God can handle the situation, whatever it may be, and if He can't, I certainly can't.

Giving God the control over an activity, a ministry, an event, or a relationship is ultimately giving Him the authority to act as He desires to act. With the authority must come the responsibility. We must also be willing to give God the responsibility for the outcome.

I remember a conversation with a minister of a large organization. He said to me, "I get up every morning knowing that I have to raise $100 million a year." When he told me that, I found myself responding, "God, I can't get into that. If You want us to grow and do more, You'll have to provide the funds." I made a decision that we weren't going to ask people for money. Rather, we were going to ask God for it. We put ourselves into a position to trust God to provide the means for the projects that He was leading us to do. Since the day we made that decision, we've been growing in our national and international ministry at a rate of about 15 percent a year, never asking anybody for a dime. I'm not taking credit for it! God is doing it. It's His work. He's responsible.

If I consider it to be my work, it becomes my responsibility. And I can't handle that responsibility!

Another part of giving God the authority and responsibility is allowing God to use other people as part of His process.When we experience burnout, we need to trust God to provide other people to fill the gaps of our inability, to take up the slack of all that we are no longer doing.

Over the years, I have discovered that if my staff and I go away for a two-day prayer retreat a couple of times a year and make key decisions together at that time, the staff can act on those decisions the rest of the time without constant input from me.

I have a weekly staff meeting that begins with prayer and lasts all Monday morning and afternoon, and that is the extent of my work each week as an administrator. I trust staff members to do their jobs and to do them truly as ministry unto the Lord.

Now, I didn't start to trust others immediately. It was a

process that took several years. I did recognize after my recovery from exhaustion that trusting others was something I had to do, and so I chose to do it. And I made a diligent effort to learn to do it.

To trust others with supervisory or administrative authority, a person must first

◆ be willing to share the glory or the credit for jobs well done.

◆ be secure, willing to let others have relationships in which the person is not a part.

◆ be willing to change the management style—to see others as people who will make mistakes occasionally rather than to dictate that no mistakes be made (which isn't possible).

Above all, it takes a willingness to see others grow in their faith and their ability to trust God to work on their behalf. I can truly say today that my foremost goal for my staff is to see each one of them believe God.

I have decided in my self that I'm going to be obedient to God, no matter what happens. But I don't take that as license to say, "Here's what we're going to do." Instead, I go into a staff meeting and say, "Here's what I've been thinking and praying about. Let's talk about it. Right or wrong, say what you are thinking." And that's the way we move toward decisions.

In going on our two-day prayer retreats, I discovered that they were far more successful if I didn't try to plan them. Originally, I'd map out the days so that we prayed all day and worked all night until midnight. We'd come home exhausted, without a lot accomplished. I felt the Lord leading me to have the staff do nothing but pray.

The first time I took the risk of leading one of these retreats without an agenda, I said to the Lord, "God, they are going to think that I came up here unprepared—that I didn't do my homework." The Lord said back in my heart, *Just trust Me.*

When I arrived, I said, "Our agenda is to pray. That's all. Just pray." Well, we prayed all morning and all afternoon. During the afternoon prayer time, a man who was in charge of all our computer operations was praying, and the Lord impressed this question on my heart, *Now, what did I say?* I thought about the Lord's words of the Great Commission—to take the gospel into all nations and make disciples. I interrupted the man in the middle of his prayer and asked him, "George, is it possible to get our In Touch program broadcast into all nations? Is that technically possible?" He said, "Yes," and then he resumed praying.

We continued to pray, and as we did, we felt the Lord calling us to get our In Touch program into every nation of the world within two years, without asking anybody for money. We left the retreat committed to that goal. We had a clear sense that the Lord had called us to do that.

Two years later, to the very week, we were broadcasting into every nation on earth.

We went on another retreat several months later, knowing that we had a great need for a building. We asked the Lord to show us what to do. We came together and really prayed and trusted God as a group.

I had a phone call when I returned home from a man in

Missouri whom I had never met. He said, "You've been on my mind the last two days. I wanted to call and tell you how much I've been blessed by your programs through the years and how much I've learned. You never talk about having any needs. I don't know if you have any or not."

I told him about our retreat and how much we were believing God to help us buy a building. He asked if we had a building in mind. I said, "Yes, we've found a building that is priced at $2.7 million, but we really felt we could buy it for $2 million."

He said, "Is it the best building for your needs?"

I said, "Yes, we believe it is. It's got everything we need."

He said, "Do you really believe you can get it for $2 million?"

I said, "Yes, I believe so."

He said, "Well, I think I can handle that."

He bought us the building outright. God had moved on his heart and met our need without our having to say a word about it!

In trusting God with both the authority to act and the responsibility for the outcome, you also need to be attuned to ways in which God may direct you to adjust the way you do various chores or routines, or the way you conduct certain aspects of your business.

The Lord led me to make some very practical changes in the way we conducted the business of the church. For example, we have a group of forty deacons at the church I pastor, and our original custom was to meet on one Monday evening of the month. The meetings would usually last for several hours. A few times, the staff and I found that they would reject something we had been working on or praying about for several weeks. I said to them, "Listen, you come in here dead tired after working all day. Without even praying about the matters we bring up, you reject them or make decisions about them. That isn't the way we should operate. Here's what I suggest: We meet on Sunday afternoon at four o'clock, and we spend the first half hour in prayer. I guarantee we'll be out of our meeting by five-thirty."

And that's what we did. We found immediately that we got more done, had greater harmony, and felt a much greater spiritual atmosphere in our meetings.

Principle #6: You ultimately must address the emotional baggage you may be carrying

We have discussed thus far principles that can help you a great deal in recovering from physical and mental burnout. I benefited from the changes I made in my schedule, my priorities, my ways of working, and my newfound ability to trust others. The root of the problem in my life, however, had not been addressed.

Although I was rested in my body, and although I had made changes to curb my striving for perfection and approval, I still felt the need for perfection and approval. A deep inner ache still filled my spirit.

Over the years—actually, over the decades—I confessed and repented ten thousand times of everything imaginable. You may ask, "Did you confess the hostility, anger, and bitterness you felt about your childhood?" Yes, I confessed all that, too, and I asked God to forgive me. I fasted, prayed, begged God, pleaded with God, cried out to God, went to seminars—you name it, I did it. Nothing satisfied the ache inside me.

If you think that praying, studying the Bible, fasting, and even working hard at sermons will make you a saint, I'm here to tell you that it doesn't work that way. Trying hard to be a Christian doesn't make you one. Trying hard to be healed of inner emotional pain won't free you from it.

Through the years, I occasionally said to Annie, "I sure would hate to die. It's not that I'm afraid to die. I'm just not ready."

One day I added, "There has to be more than I know. I have missed something. There's something I don't know that I've missed, and I've got to find out what it is." At other times I said to her, "There's something between God and me, and I just can't identify what it is. But I know there's something between us."

The ache was especially evident after I preached a series from the Bible titled "The Truth Can Set You Free." Each week of the series, people throughout the church would come up to me and say, "Pastor, these messages have really set me free."

I'd go home, however, look heavenward on Sunday afternoon, and say, "But, God, what about me? I'm the one preaching the sermon, and I don't have this freedom in my heart. I know it's Your truth, but I don't know it as a full reality in my life."

The inner pain finally grew unbearable. While I was out preaching in Oregon at a conservative Baptist meeting, everything seemed to come to a head. I would preach for about forty minutes and then quit, but the people would say, "We don't have anyplace else to go. Keep on talking." So the meetings were long, and yet God was blessing those who were there. From the outside looking in, everything seemed very successful. Yet, I went home from that conference discouraged and disheartened, and with nobody to blame. In fact, there wasn't a single thing in my life about which I could blame anybody or find fault!

Nevertheless, I was miserable to the point of being desperate. God in His mercy led me to call four friends—all of whom are very wise men, and all of whom are younger than I.

Let me share with you briefly about the hallmarks to have in seeking out a person with whom you are going to share your deepest hurts. Each man I called was qualified in these ways:

◆ *Has the person been through what you are experiencing?* Perhaps it wasn't the identical experience, but it's important that the person has felt what you are feeling and has emerged from that experience victorious, stronger, and better than ever. Such a counselor is capable of empathizing with you and truly helping you get to the answers you need. Such a counselor believes in your ultimate healing and wholeness and will hope with you for a brighter tomorrow.

◆ *Will the person speak the truth to you?* Can you trust the person to give you an honest appraisal, a sincere evaluation? A person who is employed by you, who is supervised by you, or who is in awe of you rarely will speak honestly to you.

◆ *Is the person healthy emotionally and spiritually?* Does the person's life display integrity, honesty, strength, compassion, and godly attitude and behaviors?

Then, as you receive the advice of persons with whom you share your inner pain, ask this question:

◆ *Is there an inner conviction in your spirit that the truth is being spoken to you?* The Holy Spirit bears witness with our spirits. He confirms the words of others so that we know that what we are hearing is true or untrue. A wise counselor will give you advice or make suggestions to you that ring true in your heart. If they don't, ask the Holy Spirit to show you why not. It may be that you are refusing to hear the truth. It may also be that the counselor isn't giving you the truth of God about your life.

I knew without a doubt that the four men I was calling were men of the highest integrity. They would hear me out with empathy and trust God to help them to help me.

I asked the four men if they would meet me somewhere and just let me talk to them because I was at the end of myself. I didn't know what to do, I didn't know where to go, and I didn't know to whom I could talk.

At that time in my life, I needed wise advice. And help like that frequently comes from those who see us objectively and who can help us see our lives in a new light.

The four men willingly agreed to meet with me, and we made arrangements to fly to a specific location two days later. When we had gathered together, I asked them if they would let me share with them my life. I told them that anything they advised me to do, I would do. I had that much respect for them. I conveyed to them how desperate I was. They knew I was extremely serious about receiving their counsel.

I talked with them all afternoon and all evening. I woke up several times in the middle of the night and wrote seven-

teen pages in longhand—legal-sized pages—of things I
wanted to be sure to tell them the next morning. I told them
everything I remembered about my early life and all the high-
lights—both painful and positive—of my adult life and ministry. I started with my first memory in life and brought it up
to the very moment. When I was finished, I said, "Now,
whatever you tell me to do, I'll do it."

They asked me two or three questions, and then one of
the men who was sitting directly across the table from me
said, "Charles, put your head on the table and close your
eyes." I did. He said to me very kindly, "Charles, I want you
to envision your father picking you up in his arms and holding you. What do you feel?"

I burst out crying. And I cried and I cried and I cried
and I cried. I could not stop crying. Finally, when I stopped,
he asked me again, "What do you feel?" I said, "I feel warm,
loved, secure. I feel good." And I started weeping again.

For the first time in my life, I felt emotionally that God
loved me. That may come as a shock to you. It shocked me,
too. I had known God loved me as a fact of His Word. I had
believed God loved me, accepting that as the nature of God.
But I had never emotionally felt God loving me.

For decades, I had preached about trusting God, believing God, obeying God. But when I came home and looked
through my sermon file, I discovered that I had preached only
one sermon on the love of God (and it wasn't worth listening
to). I hadn't preached on God's love because I didn't know
what it meant to feel the love of God!

God used that encounter with those four men, and that
one simple question, to begin to release me from years of

excess baggage that I had been hauling around in my life. The full release didn't happen in a day. It was a process, little by little. But the more I explored the love of God, the more God began to reveal my true identity in Christ—that I belonged to Him as I had never belonged to anybody, that I was worth something to Him (and the Cross proved that), and that He loved me beyond measure.

The chasm that had separated me from God wasn't sin. It was a chasm of damaged emotions—emotions so hurt and raw that I had been unable to experience the love of God without the help of others who saw that what I really needed was not to try harder (in fact, not to try to do anything) but, instead, to relax and feel the love of God flowing in my direction.

The first step toward getting the help you need is to admit it to someone. First and foremost, admit it to God.

Do you need help today? I've encountered many good people—including people in the ministry—who have been unable to say, "I really need help and I need it desperately." The first step toward getting the help you need is to admit it to someone. First and foremost, admit it to God. Let Him know that you are finally at the end of yourself and your efforts. It's at the point of being at the end of yourself that God can begin to do His work.

I discovered at the end of myself a kind and gracious God who had been loving me unconditionally all my life. There's nothing as liberating as that discovery! And with that discovery came an ability to help liberate others.

The more I experienced God's love in my life, the more I began to understand the importance of saying genuinely to another person, "He loves you just the way you are." I, too, came to be able to love others as they are—and to be less critical of their failed efforts or lack of perfection. God's love for me became the source of a great love for others.

That experience has affected my personal life, my ministry, my relationship with others, my family—virtually everybody I encounter.

AN INVASION OF GOD'S LOVE—AT GOD'S INITIATIVE

An amazing thing happens when we put down our emotional baggage and allow God to invade our memories. He invades our lives with His love.

For the first time in my life, I felt emotionally that God really loved me, no matter what. I felt totally accepted by Him. He had already proven to me that He was going to hang in there with me, no matter what. I had no trouble trusting God to be faithful. After that day, I had no trouble feeling that God loved me.

I had a sense of inner closeness with God that I had never experienced before. Before that time, God was always way out there. After that experience, it was as if God came all the way down from heaven and was right with me.

People may say, "Well, why didn't you feel that at the time you were saved?"

I don't know. I have asked the Lord, "Why didn't You let me experience that a long time ago?" He never answered that question. I suspect that the answer lies in the fact that I wasn't ready to receive such an outpouring of His healing, His grace, or His love. I firmly believe that God has known from the beginning of my life what He intended to do through me. And in many ways, I recognize that if I had not been through certain heartaches, trials, and failures, the message that I preach today would not be nearly as effective. There are many things I would not have understood about the extent of God's grace and mercy.

I do know this—nothing that I did to try to get close to God had worked. The feeling of closeness I feel today with God came at God's initiative.

While I prayed for the pain in my heart to be met, I recognize that He is the One who let me feel that pain.

While I prayed for direction, I recognize that He is the One who put that sense of needing direction in my heart.

While I cried out in desperation, I recognize that He is the One who led me step-by-step to that point where I would feel desperate and would cry out to Him.

Ultimately, He drew close to me in His own sovereign way, in His own timing, and for His own purposes in my life. I believe that God is always the One who takes the initiative in our lives. His longing for us is far stronger than our longing for Him. He is continually seeking a way to break through to us and let us know how much He loves us and wants close communion with us.

I could never have arranged what God has done in my life. It was entirely His orchestration.

Once established, intimacy with God grows. The outpouring of His love that I felt just those few short years ago has continued to grow, and it grows not in spite of the struggles, problems, joys, and sorrows of life but out of them. My greatest desire today is to become more and more intimate with God. There's nothing in life that I want more than that. To me, that is the most exciting possibility that life holds. God is infinite, and we are finite: therefore, the capacity for God's intimacy with us can never reach an end. There's always some way in which we can become more intimate with Him if we are willing to receive His embrace extended toward us.

TRUTH CAPSULE

When you are feeling burned out . . .

1. Put yourself into a position to rest. Get away. Take a long enough break for your body to mend, your mind to clear, and your heart to heal.

2. Ask the Lord to show you how to trust Him more. Ask Him to reveal to you specific ways in which you can turn over the authority and responsibility of your life to Him. Ask Him to give you specific ways in which you can lighten the load of your schedule and obligations.

3. Admit to the Lord that you are responsible for your burnout tendencies. Ask the Lord to show you what to do about the inner pain and emotional baggage that may be driving you to strive relentlessly for approval and perfection. Ask the Lord to do whatever is necessary in your life for you to get to the place and time where He can heal you and fill your life with His approval, His love, and His presence.

My excess baggage from burnout.

_____

_____

_____

_____

_____

_____

_____

_____

_____

How I can lighten this load.

_____

_____

_____

_____

_____

_____

_____

_____

_____

God is the source of my strength.

*Words
of
comfort
and
healing
to
those
who
are
being*

PERSECUTED

8

*H*ow can you keep your balance in the midst of a situation that is abusive and painful—a situation in which you know with certainty that God intends for you to stay and for which there seems to be no resolution?

Such a situation can best be described as persecution, especially when you are receiving the abuse because of your witness for the Lord and your behaviors that are based on biblical standards.

I **knew that I could retaliate directly or I could pray. I chose to pray.** ◆

Persecution is the very situation I faced prior to my being called as the senior pastor of First Baptist Church in Atlanta.

When I arrived in Atlanta, I discovered that nobody in the church other than the executive committee even knew I was coming. I was introduced to the church on a Sunday morning by a man who said simply, "I want you to meet our new associate pastor, Charles Stanley. He's going to preach for us this morning." The brevity of his introduction didn't bother me at all. I just stood up and preached.

During the first year and a half I was there, apart from Sunday morning services, I saw the senior pastor only three times. The executive committee ran the church.

The time came when the senior pastor invited a man to preach a week-long revival at the church, and in a nutshell, nothing happened. Now, it was a Baptist revival, so surely somebody ought to have been saved! On Sunday morning, the senior pastor preached, and still, nobody came forward. He said, "This is so sickening, I can't stand it." And he threw the microphone down on the platform and walked out. That was the beginning of the end for him in that church. A short time later, he resigned.

As associate pastor, I had the primary responsibility of preaching on Sunday nights. With the senior pastor gone, I also was asked to preach on Sunday mornings. Things started happening. More people began coming to the services. People were getting saved. A new atmosphere was taking hold in the church.

The executive committee continued to run the business of the church. I met with them one day on a business matter, and as we were facing the decision before us, I said, "We need to ask God about this." The businessmen looked at one another and then at me, and they said, "Let's leave God out of this. This is business." I said, "Oh, we can't do that." That, no doubt, was the first sign they saw that I wasn't going to be easy to control.

The pulpit committee of forty had a core group called the executive committee, made up of the most influential and wealthy members of the church. Those seven decided they just couldn't handle the idea of my ever becoming the senior pastor, so they began to lobby the other members of the pulpit committee to turn me down as a candidate for the position.

After about three months of their lobbying, I finally realized what was happening. I knew that I could retaliate directly or I could pray. I chose to pray.

You see, I had a certainty in my heart that I was to be the senior pastor of the First Baptist Church in Atlanta. While in West Palm Beach to preach a revival, I was praying on Friday afternoon, and the Lord spoke in my heart and said, *Here's what I am going to do.* He outlined His plan for me in Atlanta.

It's one thing to know God's will. It's another thing, however, to do God's will in the face of people who don't want you to do it!

I'd go into the prayer room at the church, think about the situation I was facing, and say, "God, there's no way." And time and again He'd speak back in my heart, *Just trust Me. Don't look around. Trust Me. Don't listen to what people are saying. Trust Me!* Each time, I'd say back to Him, "God, I trust You."

Every Sunday morning I'd go into my prayer room off my study and get down on my face before God and say, "I want to walk out to the pulpit full of Your Spirit and Your power." And every Sunday, God empowered me to do just that. I preached as if nothing had been said against me all week. However, rumors and false accusations were flying everywhere.

One of the main accusations against me was that all I preached was salvation, the Holy Spirit, and the second coming of Christ. That wasn't all I had preached on, but that was

It's one thing to know God's will. It's another thing, however, to do God's will in the face of people who don't want you to do it!

all they had heard. Most people who opposed me had serious qualms about the authenticity of the Bible and its applicability to our day and time.

If you take away human need and God's provision for salvation, the work of the Holy Spirit, the hope of the second coming of Christ, and the validity of the Bible as the authoritative Word of God, what do you have in a church? You don't really have a church. You have a social club. And that's what had developed and what was at issue. The matter was a spiritual battle, nothing less.

At the outset, the main body of the congregation didn't know about the false accusations that were being spread about me. They just responded to the Word of God.

Slowly, however, the words against me began to infiltrate the congregation. I remember one man who stood one week and gave testimony, saying, "I've learned more about the Word of God in the last six months than in my entire life." The next week, he wouldn't even speak to me. People who greeted me warmly one week wouldn't even look my way the next Sunday.

The goal of the core committee of seven men was to convince at least twenty-one of the forty members of the larger committee not to vote for me as the senior pastor. Simple majority ruled. I could never figure out why those people didn't go out and find another senior pastor. Instead, they concentrated on defaming me, as if somehow I was standing in the way of their calling another man. The reality of the matter was that I was only an interim pastor, and technically, I was still the associate pastor. Their only attempt at finding someone else was to talk to a man who was extremely liberal and to promise him the moon if he came. When word got out to the rest of the committee members about it, they came unglued.

One day I was invited to lunch by two members of the core group of seven with the intent that they were going to make me an offer that included my leaving on vacation and never returning. I said to them, "I didn't come to this church because you called me. I came because God called me to come here. I'll be happy to leave the minute God tells me to leave."

Shortly after that encounter, three members of the committee invited me to lunch with the same intent. Two of the three didn't show up. The third man—a man I had come to love dearly—began to talk cautiously about a cash offer the committee was willing to make if I would leave the church quietly and quickly.

I looked him in the eye and said, "If you don't know me any better than that after these two years, you really don't know me. You couldn't stack up enough money on this table to cause me to deliberately and willfully disobey God. Go back to those who sent you and tell them, 'No deal.' Any deal they make will have to be with God."

The conflict went on for ten months. During that time, I came to feel like a stranger in my church. Virtually all of the staff members turned against me. The only allies I felt I had were ten women who met regularly with my wife to pray for me.

While I was at Bryan College preaching one week, the vote was made by the deacons, and then by the committee of forty, that I not be called to be the pastor. The committee and deacons were fully prepared to make a negative recommendation to the congregation.

Meanwhile, I was up at Bryan, attempting to prepare the Sunday morning sermon. I knew it was going to be one of the most important sermons of my life—I would preach it the Sunday morning prior to the Wednesday night at which the congregation would vote on whether I should be called as the senior pastor.

No sermon ideas surfaced. I returned to Atlanta without a sermon idea. I didn't even have a Scripture to preach on! Saturday night I went to bed, still with no sermon, and I prayed, "God, I don't have a thing to say tomorrow morning." On Sunday morning, I awoke and still no sermon. I said, "Now, God, I haven't said a word about this entire conflict, and I'm not about to start now."

I went to my study at the church and scratched out a little outline just in case. But I thought, *No, I've trusted God to give me my sermons all these years, and I'm not going to start trusting myself now.* I crumpled up that outline, threw it in the trash, and walked out to the sanctuary. The service began. The choir started to sing. Still no sermon. I said under my breath, "God, this is all Yours because I don't have a thing to say."

When the choir finished, I walked up to the pulpit and let my Bible fall open wherever it would. It opened to Proverbs 3:5–6:

> Trust in the LORD with all your heart,
> And lean not on your own understanding;
> In all your ways acknowledge Him,
> And He shall direct your paths.

It was as if God pulled me away and said, *Now, watch this.* For forty minutes, His words on obedience to God came streaming out of me. I had no notes, but I could hardly catch my breath between sentences. The flow of God's Word was nonstop until I concluded that sermon. I gave the invitation to come forward for salvation. People in the choir began getting up and walking out the side exits. People in the congregational area began getting up and walking out the back door. A third group was coming down the aisle to get saved. The people who were walking out of the church and the people who were coming forward to get saved were passing each other in the aisles.

It was a total division of the house!

On Wednesday afternoon, just hours before the congregational vote, three lawyers came to see me to tell me why I couldn't be the pastor, how the church would never accept me, how my future as a minister was over if the church voted me out, and how I'd never get another job.

I said to them, "You're asking me to make a decision I have to live with the rest of my life. I'm putting that decision back on you and on the congregation. You and they are going to have to make a decision that you will live with the rest of your lives. I'm willing to abide by your decision because I know God will take care of me. But I can't disobey God and leave this place until He tells me to go. I'm willing to live with my decision if you're willing to live with yours. If the people in this church vote to fire me, that's fine. But that will be their decision, not mine."

Wednesday night came. Annie and I slipped in and sat

in the back of one of the side wings. The moderator did not know we were there.

I sat there with my Bible opened to Isaiah 54:17,

"No weapon formed against you shall prosper,
And every tongue which rises
    against you in judgment
You shall condemn.
This is the heritage of the
    servants of the LORD,
And their righteousness is from Me,"
Says the LORD.

I said, "God, there's nothing I can do about what happens here tonight. This is totally in Your hands."

The meeting was led by the chairman of the board of deacons (which had voted for me to leave). As a part of his opening remarks, he said, "We'll vote by secret ballot." At that, a man stood up toward the back of the auditorium and said, "No, we're not! Tonight we're going to find out where everybody stands. I make a motion that we vote by a standing vote on every measure." His motion was seconded, and it passed.

The meeting went on for three hours. When the members of the opposition realized that things were not going their way, they did everything they could do to end the meeting and postpone the vote on my leadership. The amazing thing to me was that in all that time, not one person stood and gave a reason for not wanting me to be the pastor.

Finally, Mrs. Sauls—a lovely woman who had been a

nurse for some fifty years—stood and said in her sweet southern drawl, "Mr. Chairman, I call for the question." When the
two thousand people there that night were put to a vote,
about two-thirds stood in favor of my being the pastor; about
one-third stood in opposition. It was a clear decision.

After the vote was taken, a man noticed that I was
present, and he asked me to come down to the platform. I
acted as if the vote had been unanimous in my favor, and I
said, "I appreciate your confidence. I'll give you an answer in
two weeks."

I spent those two weeks in prayer to make certain that
the word the Lord had given me in West Palm Beach was still
His word to me. I had the full confidence that it was, and I
accepted the call to be the senior pastor.

The people who had opposed me so vigorously never
came back to church. They began meeting in a medical building a couple of blocks away. Oh, they came to Sunday school,
but after Sunday school, they'd walk down the street to their
service. They also came on Wednesday evenings to eat in the
dining room, but after supper, they refused to come to the
prayer meeting.

That went on for three months. Then one day in Janu-
ary, the Lord laid Psalm 64 on my heart, especially verse 7:

But God shall shoot at them with an arrow;
Suddenly they shall be wounded.

The next Wednesday night, which was a business meeting, I asked the church to give my Sunday school superinten-
dent and me the full authority to appoint all the deacons and

all the church officers. A member of the original opposition stood and gave a speech about how we were running him out of the church, and then he said, "If you don't watch what you're doing, you're going to get hurt." With that, he hit me with the back of his hand in the face.

A woman stood and said, "How dare you hit my pastor!" Another man, a former boxer, rushed up on the platform, and even though he was about seventy years old, he held out his cane (which had a brass head) and said, "You're not going to hit my pastor!" Another friend also jumped up on the platform and escorted away the man who had hit me.

I didn't say a word. I didn't even register a reaction. I knew in my heart, however, that Psalm 64:7 had just been executed by God. The man's actions had made the entire opposition appear to be a group that couldn't control itself.

Some of the people in the congregation began to cry. When the vote was taken, my request to name the deacons and officers of the church passed.

The next Sunday on the way to church my wife, Annie, gave me this Scripture: God said to Moses, "The Egyptians whom you see today, you shall see again no more forever. The LORD will fight for you, and you shall hold your peace" (Exod. 14:13–14).

During the Sunday morning service, we began singing the first song, and a man came rushing up to the platform, pushed away the song leader, and said, "Today, you haven't come to hear a sermon. You've come to witness a funeral."

I motioned to our television cameramen to turn off the cameras. The man continued to talk, and as he did, three people stood and began to sing "Onward, Christian Soldiers."

The rest of the congregation stood and joined them in singing. The man left. The people remained like a solid wall.

A woman who had been watching us on television saw the man rush up to the pulpit before the cameras went to black, and she called the police and said, "There's a long-bearded hippie trying to take over the service at the Baptist church." Several police cars arrived on our doorstep. It was quite a day.

The next night, thirty of the sixty deacons resigned. On Tuesday morning, all of the Women's Missionary Union leaders resigned, and over half of the Sunday school teachers resigned. When the opposition finally left, the rest of the church had a party to celebrate their leaving.

In the wake of their leaving, the opposition made a vow to our television station that they would interrupt every service thereafter unless the station took us off the air. The station complied, and for one year (to the day), we were off television. What happened during the following year? The church began to grow rapidly. And when we went back on the air, we returned with programs on two stations. (Furthermore, those programs were in color; our previous program had been in black and white.)

It was as if all the old dead wood had been cut away and the church pruned back so it could explode with growth and spiritual blessing.

The thing that personally hurt me the most through the experience was a feeling of rejection by some people I had thought were my friends and colleagues.

On the Monday after I had accepted the congregation's vote to be their pastor, I held a staff meeting and said, "You

It was as if all the old dead wood had been cut away and the church pruned back so it could explode with growth and spiritual blessing.

all have the privilege of resigning if you like." All but two resigned. John Glover, the music minister, wanted to leave but felt God telling him to stay. John has now been with me more than twenty years. The other staff member who stayed was Mary Gellerstedt. She worked with me until she retired.

WHAT ARE GOD'S PRINCIPLES FOR DEALING WITH PERSECUTION?

One day as I was praying about the persecution I was receiving, I felt the Lord impress on my heart, *Take this as if it's coming from Me.*

That word from the Lord changed my perspective on everything I was hearing and experiencing. When people said things to me, I'd immediately say to the Lord in my spirit, "What is it that You are trying to tell me, Lord? What message are You wanting me to receive? How are You directing me to pray?" I saw people as being instruments in God's hands. I saw them as having no authority of their own. I was in touch with the true Power of the church, the One who was allowing them to exert a little noise but who would never relinquish His authority over His church!

I discovered four vital keys to dealing with persecution during those difficult months at the church.

Key #1: Keep your eyes on the Lord

When I got my eyes off the Lord and onto my persecutors, I found myself feeling anger, bitterness, and resentment toward them and toward life in general. When I saw my abusers as part of a greater lesson that God was teaching me and a greater work that He was doing in my life—and that God was doing only what was going to result in my eternal good—I felt peace. Yes, I even felt love toward those who were persecuting me.

The Lord said, *If you see what is happening as something that I'm allowing in order to develop you into an even stronger, more victorious person, you'll come out of this not bitter, but better!*

Some people consider that all forms of persecution come from the devil. In one regard, they are correct. God never instigates, authorizes, or promotes persecution. On the other hand, God does allow persecution to come our way. We see this clearly in the life of Job in the Bible. God did not authorize the devil's persecution of Job, but He did allow the devil to test him and to bring situations in his life that might well be described as abusive.

What was God's purpose in the life of Job? One of His purposes was to win a battle against the devil. Job's faithfulness and refusal to sin were victories for God over the devil. The Lord also used the devil's persecution in Job's personal life to prepare Job for even greater revelations of Himself.

In nearly every incident of persecution I've witnessed, I have seen God's purposes at work in much the same way. When a victim remains faithful to the Lord and refuses to sin, God gains a victory over the devil. The power of the devil is thwarted; his influence is diminished; a greater strength emerges—not only in the righteous victim but in those who witness the actions of the righteous victim.

At the same time, when a victim turns to the Lord for help, sustenance, and wisdom, the Lord has an opportunity to

When a victim remains faithful to the Lord and refuses to sin, God gains a victory over the devil.

reveal Himself to that victim as He never has before. He gives greater insights into His nature, His purposes on this earth, and the relationship He desires to have with the person. The Lord often causes the victim to have a deeper awareness of personal value to Him, and of the Lord's presence and power always.

Key #2: Ask the Lord to sustain you and strengthen you

The Bible has much to say about those who endure.

The victor's crown goes to those who run the race all the way to the end.

The reward of God is given to those who withstand the evil day.

The blessing of God is granted to those who overcome and who stand firm in their faith.

If you are experiencing persecution, ask the Lord to sustain you in it, to help you not to sin—or to become weak-hearted or fearful—and to show you how you must respond so that He receives glory and honor. Ask the Lord to reveal Himself to you as your Victor, Savior, and Deliverer.

Key #3: Recognize that you are fighting a spiritual battle

To be able to withstand persecution, you must know with certainty that the battle is the Lord's—that you are being persecuted for the cause of Christ, and not simply for an act of your foolishness, error, or stubbornness.

Ask yourself,

◆ "Has the Lord really directed me to take the stance for which I am being persecuted?"

◆ "Am I being persecuted for His name's sake or my reputation?"

◆ "What is at stake here? Is the kingdom of God going to be advanced by a victory, or will only my personal career and reputation be advanced? Is the kingdom of God truly going to suffer a blow, or a loss, in a defeat?"

Perhaps the most potent question you can ask is a tough one: "Who will get the glory for a victory?" If the person who is applauded for the victory is anyone other than the Lord Jesus Christ, mixed motives are in play. To God be the glory for a victory over persecutors and to no one else! After all, it is His glory that is being attacked.

True persecution is always related to the Lord's cause or the Lord's work. It has a spiritual root. As such, we must always deal with it in a spiritual manner.

In fighting a spiritual battle, we do well to remind our-selves of Paul's words to the Ephesians:

> Be strong in the Lord and in the power of His might. Put on the whole armor of God, that you may be able to stand against the wiles of the devil. For we do not wrestle against flesh and blood, but against principalities, against powers, against the rulers of the darkness of this age, against spiritual hosts of wickedness in the heavenly places. Therefore take up the whole armor of God, that you may be able to withstand in the evil day, and having done all, to

Perhaps the most potent question you can ask is a tough one: "Who will get the glory for a victory?"

stand. Stand therefore, having girded your waist with truth, having put on the breastplate of righteousness, and having shod your feet with the preparation of the gospel of peace; above all, taking the shield of faith with which you will be able to quench all the fiery darts of the wicked one. And take the helmet of salvation, and the sword of the Spirit, which is the word of God; praying always with all prayer and supplication in the Spirit, being watchful to this end with all perseverance and supplication for all the saints (6:10–18).

Notice in summary what Paul commands the Ephesians to do:

1. Arm yourself with the truth. Make sure you know the truth of the situation from God's perspective.
2. Arm yourself with righteousness. Make certain that you are in right standing with God and that you are living a blameless life before your persecutors. Their persecution of you gives you no license to sin.
3. Arm yourself with God's peace. Make peace your goal—a peace that means a true reconciliation of your enemies to God, not merely a truce with you. Always use the gospel of the Lord to speak encouragement to your persecutors, not to inflame or incite the anger of those who are opposing you or abusing you.

4. Arm yourself with faith. Keep your focus on the Lord Jesus.
5. Arm yourself with the confidence of your salvation and deliverance at God's hand. Expect the victory that's coming! Count on it as a certainty.
6. Arm yourself with the Word of God. Be quick to speak the Word of God in the midst of your persecution. Let God's Word do your talking for you.
7. Having done all to arm yourself, endure in prayer. Pray for those who are persecuting you. Pray for God to move on their hearts and to save them. Pray for your fellow believers that God will strengthen them as they stand with you in your time of persecution.
8. Finally, being fully armed and in prayer, persevere. Don't give up. Don't give in. In fact, don't give an inch! Hang tough for the Lord.

In centuries past, when great sailing ships traversed the oceans of the world and the prediction of storms was not based on satellite photos and the instant communication systems we have today, ships frequently were engulfed by fierce storms. Sailors, and even captains of ships, would bind themselves to the ship's masts to keep from being swept overboard by giant waves that threatened to capsize the vessel. In that manner, they'd ride out the storm, trusting God to calm the winds and waves.

When the storms of abuse rage against us—and we find ourselves sailing in waters where we know the Lord has led us

—we must do likewise. We must bind ourselves to the mast of the Lord Jesus and hold tight, trusting God to rebuke the storm that is raging against us and, at the same time, preserve our lives, strengthen us in His goodness, and keep us strong in our faith.

When the storms of abuse rage against us—and we find ourselves sailing in waters where we know the Lord has led us—we must bind ourselves to the mast of the Lord Jesus and hold tight.

Key #4: Keep looking for the victory

Never lose sight of the goal, the reason you are enduring the pain and rejection you may be experiencing. Much is at stake.

Jesus taught,

> Blessed are those who are persecuted for righteousness' sake, for theirs is the kingdom of heaven. Blessed are you when they revile and persecute you, and say all kinds of evil against you falsely for My sake. Rejoice and be exceedingly glad, for great is your reward in heaven (Matt. 5:10–12).

The kingdom of heaven is to be gained through your persecution. Not only that, but a great reward within the kingdom of heaven is yours!

My friend, there's no comparison between the temporary, earthly, transient anger of persecutors and the glory of eternity. Persecution is but for a season. As painful as a persecutor's accusations may be, they are as words evaporating in the wind. What is persecution by others compared to eternal rewards and the assurance that you will be a resident of the kingdom of heaven forever?

In addition to the rewards of eternity, the Lord has benefits for us here on this earth. The persecutions that we experience

◆ strengthen us in our faith.

◆ toughen us in our resolve to win souls.

◆ cause a refinement of our souls.

◆ give us greater and greater cause to praise His name.

The scars of the faithful are acquired in persecution.

We must always be on the alert for what God is doing in our lives—the lessons He is teaching us, the experiences He is causing us to have so that we might be conformed more and more to the image of His Son, Christ Jesus, and the victories He is allowing us to have so that we might be ever stronger soldiers in His army of the faithful. We grow through persecution.

That being the case, if you are experiencing persecution for the Lord's sake, dig in your heels, hang on, cling to Jesus, and endure until the Lord gives the victory!

TRUTH CAPSULE

When you are feeling persecuted . . .

1. Evaluate your position. Make certain before the Lord that you are truly being persecuted for His sake and not for your sake. If you are truly facing persecution for the Lord's cause, the next points apply.

2. Count yourself privileged. The Lord is trusting you to win a spiritual battle.

3. Fight your persecutors in the Lord. Arm yourself for a spiritual battle, and begin to intercede for the good of God's people.

4. Choose, as an act of your will, to endure until the Lord gives the victory.

*M*y excess baggage from persecution.

_____

_____

_____

_____

_____

_____

_____

_____

_____

*H*ow I can lighten this load.

_____

_____

_____

_____

_____

_____

_____

_____

_____

*G*od is the source of my strength.

The Purifying Power of Pain

*P*ain can have a purifying power in our lives in that it drives us toward the Lord and His healing power. Emotional pain is relentless.

It nags.

It gnaws.

It festers.

It stays with us until we deal with it.

Oh, we may attempt to deny our emotional pain or to sublimate it. All we really succeed in doing, however, is to push the pain deeper into our spirits. To be truly healed of our pain, we must face it, take it to the Lord, let Him begin a healing work in us, and then choose to live in accordance with what He tells us to do.

The good news is that when the Lord begins to do a healing work in us, that work purifies us. The dregs of our painful past—the emotional garbage that has been fermenting in us—are washed away. Our minds and hearts are cleansed. We are then able to regain our balance. Our strength is renewed. And we can go forward in life with new vigor.

It is vitally important for us to recognize that a continuing or lingering emotional pain is a signal to us from the Lord. It is a message that He wants to do something in our lives—that He isn't content for us to carry that weight, or that emotional baggage, in our hearts any longer. Emotional pain can, and must, be seen as an initiative from God that will draw us to Him so that He may heal us.

Our failures and our hurts can be a key to discovering who God wants us to be. Trauma, grief, and crisis can be the launching pads that move us from one level of personal spiritual growth to another. That doesn't mean we need to seek out trauma, grief, and crisis. The Bible tells us that in this life we will have tribulation. The challenge we face is in how we choose to respond to those times. Will we turn to God? Will we allow God to minister to our need? Will we trust Him and let Him use those difficult circumstances to create growth in us? Will we be open to the changes He wants to make in our lives?

God's part is to initiate a closer relationship with us. Our part is to choose to respond correctly to God's initiative. If I don't choose to respond to God, and if I choose instead to turn to drugs, crime, or some other means of reacting, there's nothing that God will do to override the willful negative response.

When I look back on my life, I'm grateful for the times when I chose to respond to God's initiative to the best that I was capable of responding. It's when we willfully turn away from God or seek solutions in other places that God cannot break through to us. What an irony it is that many people who do not respond to God blame God for being unresponsive to them or even try to blame Him for the bad things that

> God's part is to initiate a closer relationship with us. Our part is to choose to respond correctly to God's initiative.

happen in their lives! Our response must always be toward God, not away from Him.

CHOOSE TODAY TO TURN TO GOD

Choose to turn to His Word. No matter what I'm feeling—good or bad, discouraged or encouraged—I turn to the Word of God for advice about why I'm feeling that way. The more miserable I feel, the more I turn to God's Word. I have to trust God to reveal to me His answers through His Word. I'm always learning something new. I always have fresh insight to ponder and digest. I have a strong sense that God is continually at work transforming more and more of my life into the image of His Son, Jesus Christ.

It's important as we turn to God's Word that we turn to the whole of God's Word. Many times people want something so desperately that they go to the Bible and find one or two verses that convince them that it is God's will that they have that thing, and then in their own words, they stand on those verses. To me, that is not a true exercise of faith.

I believe a better approach is to say, "Father, I give myself to You. You know who I am and what is in my best interest. I'm trusting You to give me the things I need and to give me those things that are truly going to be of benefit to me."

The Lord's best for you is going to be better than anything you can choose! The Lord is going to give you only the best for you.

If you take this approach—trusting God to provide for

The Lord's best for you is going to be better than anything you can choose!

you the best of everything that He knows you need—you will
be freed in four ways:

1. You'll know that whatever comes your way is
   truly from the Lord. You'll never have cause to
   confuse what is of your own engineering and
   what is a gracious gift from God.
2. You'll be freed from striving for things—from
   planning and struggling and scheming day in and
   day out to get the things you need or want. You'll
   be freed of all need to manipulate your circumstances.
3. You'll be freed from all concern about whether
   you've made the right choices or you've settled for
   something that is less than God's best.
4. You'll be freed in your ability to praise God, for
   you'll see His provisions and His providence far
   more clearly. You'll know that He, and He alone,
   is the Source of your total supply.

A DAILY WALK OF FAITH

The Christian life is to be lived day by day. If you have
your mind continually engaged in thinking about your long-
range goals or ways in which you can achieve, earn, or have
something way out yonder, you'll miss many of today's blessings. You'll be less able to enjoy the relationships and good
things that God has given you to enjoy right now. You may
miss the very thing that would satisfy you the most!

The same thing holds for your emotions. If you are continually living in old emotions—feelings and reactions that you have had for many years, old hurts, or festering wounds—you will miss out on the joys of responding to today.

When the Bible says, "The just shall live by faith" (Hab. 2:4; Rom. 1:17; Heb. 10:38), it means precisely what we are talking about—that those who are truly in right standing with God live with their faith fully activated in a living God, who is going to lead them into right paths, give them the best blessings, provide for them all that they need, and reveal to them the deepest and most meaningful insights into His Word and His ways.

To live by faith on a daily basis, you need to deal with emotional hurts as they come your way. You must take each thought captive. You must feel each feeling. You must repent quickly of each sin. Don't let yourself stuff emotions, thoughts, or sins into the deep recesses of your spirit to deal with them later. Deal with them even now.

My conscience is like a razor. I can't go to bed at night if there's something between God and me. Even if I'm in a struggle where I don't know what is going on, I have to deal with that struggle to the best of my ability every day. I have to reach conclusions and make decisions about that struggle before the day ends.

If you are experiencing a bout of loneliness, go to God immediately about that feeling.

If you are feeling rejected or hurt, run to the throne room of God and ask Him to help you.

If you are feeling frustrated, angry, bitter, or resent-

Don't let yourself stuff emotions, thoughts, or sins into the deep recesses of your spirit to deal with them later. Deal with them even now.

ful, ask for God's help as soon as you experience that feeling.

In giving our emotions to God on a moment-by-moment, day-by-day basis, we put ourselves into a position for Him to reveal Himself to us and to give us His power and presence in an ongoing way. We truly put ourselves into a position of trusting Him to lead us, guide us, and heal us continually.

Our intimacy grows with the Lord as a result of that kind of faith walk. The more intimate we become with God, the more we're able to trust Him. That's true for every relationship, isn't it? The closer you draw to a person, and the more you rely upon that person, and the more you experience the trustworthiness of that person, the more you trust that person. The more you trust a person and share your life with that person, the closer you feel to that person. Trust and intimacy are very closely related.

The more intimate I become with God, the better I understand Him, the more clearly I see the relationship He desires to have with me, the more accurately I discern what His interests are and what He is desiring to do, and the more I trust His motives and His ability to accomplish His purposes in my life.

EMOTIONAL HEALING TAKES TIME

The healing of emotional pain takes time. God could do the healing work in an instant. But generally, we need time to absorb His healing work, to understand His work in our lives, and to alter our thought patterns. We can know with certainty that

♦ God begins the healing work in us instantly, the moment we request His presence and ask Him to do His work within us.

♦ God will be faithful to continue the healing process in us as long as we are willing for Him to do so. Philippians 1:6 declares, "He who has begun a good work in you will complete it until the day of Jesus Christ." God doesn't give up on you. He will work with you to heal you completely. He will stand by you and be faithful in His relationship with you until you are fully healed of the emotional pain you feel.

The more we are healed emotionally, the softer we become emotionally. We become more tolerant and sensitive. When that happens, we are in a position to become agents of healing to others.

God will stand by you and be faithful in His relationship with you until you are fully healed of the emotional pain you feel.

RUN TO THE LORD TODAY

Let your pain drive you to God today.

In running to God and in resting in Him, you will discover more about who He is. You will discover more about who He has created you to be, how He desires that you relate to others, and what is truly valuable and important in life. If you let your pain drive you to God, you will discover what is important to God.

And ultimately, you will be healed of your pain. The Lord desires to bind up the brokenhearted. Invite Him to do His work in you today.

Charles Stanley is heard nationally and internationally on the In Touch television and radio broadcasts. His messages cover a broad range of topics. The following is a list of messages relevant to *The Source of My Strength*:

Advancing Through Adversity
Dealing with Life's Pressures
Forgiveness, God's Grace Demonstrated
God's Love—Your Ultimate Security
How to Handle Your Emotions
How the Truth Can Set You Free
Living Above Our Circumstances
Living Triumphantly Through Our Trials
Our Unmet Needs
The God who Cares
True Peace

These messages and others are available on audiotape and videotape. To purchase a tape or to obtain a complete list of products available, call In Touch Ministries at 1-800-323-3747 or write to:

In Touch Ministries
P.O. Box 7900
Atlanta, Georgia 30357

Other books by Charles Stanley

How to Listen to God
How to Keep Your Kids on Your Team
Winning the War Within
The Gift of Forgiveness
Eternal Security
The Wonderful Spirit-Filled Life

These books are available at your local bookstore.